THE UNINTENTIONAL INTERIM

THE UNINTENTIONAL INTERIM

Ministry in Times of Transition

Jeffrey A. Nelson

The Pilgrim Press, 1300 East 9th Street
Cleveland, Ohio 44114
thepilgrimpress.com

Published 2025.

Printed on acid-free paper.

Library of Congress Cataloging-in-Publication Data on file.
LCCN: 2024931014

ISBN 978-0-8298-0128-6 (paper)
ISBN 978-0-8298-0129-3 (ebook)

Printed in The United States of America.

WITH GRATITUDE

for the lives and ministries of

Rev. Jerry Baker

Rev. Jane Heckles

and Rev. Rich Plant

CONTENTS

First Things

I want to begin with a disclaimer. This is a ministry book that does not purport to offer concrete solutions to what you may be facing. So many do (purport, that is, not offer), and I don't want to get your hopes up.

What I do want to offer are tools that may aid you in finding solutions for your particular context and all of its unique variables. We are in a time in which most are still discovering actual solutions with limited success. But if we are equipped with some solid ideas about where to direct our attention, such solutions are more likely to arise. Whether they are easily transferable from one ministry context to another—again, as many other ministry books suggest they should be—is a suggestion that this book will not make, because I am not confident that it is possible. Let's just say that during my years as a pastor, I lost too many illusions to continue believing otherwise. Maybe you have as well.

That said, here is where we will travel over the course of this book.

Chapter 1 attempts to summarize the moment. It gives an overview of the many transitional needs facing the church, as well as defining the concept of "unintentional interim" and its relevance for these times.

The next three chapters analyze different pieces of the experience of ministry in transition. First, chapter 2 engages with disillusionment and attempts to reclaim it from its negative connotations. Chapter 3 explores the ongoing effect that negative expectations may have on one's mind and spirit. Chapter 4 examines the effects of grief in congregations that have not yet made peace with a past ending.

Chapter 5 explores the earliest days of the Interim Ministry Network and its important work toward defining the role of the intentional interim minister, as well as how we may need to revisit its proposed "five developmental tasks" in light of current circumstances.

Chapter 6 discusses the importance of having a strong network of support both inside and outside the congregation. Thankfully, ministers do not seem to be as prone to playing the part of the Lone Ranger the way they might have in years past. But identifying these individuals and groups will still be important.

Chapter 7 analyzes the experience of dealing with failure. It does so through an invitation to reframe it by considering how factors outside of one's control play much more of a role than we may be able to acknowledge in the moment. Any minister is entering a congregation in one part of a long story that was happening before and will continue after.

Chapters 8 and 9 deal with different aspects of the minister's need to tend to their own well-being. First, we look at practices for caring for one's mental, physical, spiritual, and creative health. Then we explore the typical cycle of discernment from its highest points of affirmation to its lowest of evaluating whether to opt out.

Finally, chapter 10 thematizes our needs to seek resurrection in the midst of a moment that feels much more like Holy Saturday: a time when signs of new life seem scarce if they seem present at all.

The end of each chapter invites readers to observe a journaling exercise. These include an opening and closing breath exercise to center you for the practice and several prompts to prayerfully reflect on your own experience of each chapter's subject matter. You don't need to be an experienced journal keeper to do this, nor do you need a top-of-the-line journal. A lined notebook from any corner store will suffice, along with a simple willingness to give it a try. These are included as one possible avenue to explore your sense of ministry.

The notion of keeping a journal while reading this book may be intimidating or off-putting based on past experience or on a general wariness of the practice: you might wonder whether you'll be able to stick with it, or writing may not be your primary method of processing your thoughts. I suggest this practice as a way to keep track of your reflections as you read, as well as to revisit them the further you go. You'll be able to build upon or change your mind about earlier writing as you continue to ponder your own experience of the topics discussed.

In many chapters, I share my story of what I perceived to be ministry in an unintentional interim situation. In some ways, it is not typical: I was fortunate enough to stay for much longer than such a pastorate often lasts, and overall my time there was mild in comparison to other situations in congregations that can be much more resistant, if not outright mean. That was not the nature of this particular scenario, but it meets the criteria in other ways.

I have removed most descriptive details of those involved because I am more concerned with sharing how the elements of change, grief, pastoral care, and moving a congregation toward a new beginning played out. I am sharing my story without malice or resentment, and I have done my best to present it in that spirit. My intent is to show how these factors played out in one instance among many.

No matter the kind of transitions you are currently called to minister through, I hope you find a few tools in this book that will help you discover the solutions that you and your context need.

the practice, you might wonder whether you'll be able to stick with it or whether it might be your primary method of processing [illegible]. I suggest this practice as a way to keep track of your reflections as you read, as well as a way to share them [illegible] with others [illegible] upon [illegible] [illegible] your own experience of the topic [illegible].

In many chapters I share my story of what I personally faced in ministry in an interim or urgent situation. In some ways, it is not typical. I was fortunate enough to stay for much longer than [illegible], and overall my experience was mild in comparison to other situations, interims that can be much more resistant. [illegible] that was not the nature of this particular church, but it has its difficulties in other ways.

I [illegible] most descriptive details of those involved because I am more concerned with sharing the effects of change [illegible] and maybe a congregation toward a new beginning played out [illegible] story [illegible] I have done my best to [illegible] in a [illegible] spirit. My intention is to show how these factors played out [illegible] among many.

No matter the kind of transitions you are currently called to minister through, I hope you find a few tools in this book that will help you discover the sacred that surround your ministry.

We Are All Interims Now

In the spring of 2012, I began paying attention to some internal stirrings regarding the state of my ministry at a small rural church in northeast Ohio. It seemed to me that the time was right to begin a season of evaluation and discernment, and to explore the possibility that I might be called away from that congregation to begin a new ministry elsewhere. I had been serving with this church for nearly eight years at this point. Our time together had been productive and full of spiritual and missional growth, and we enjoyed a strong mutual relationship. But I felt as if I had reached a point where staying further might lead to stagnation for both of us, and I wanted to avoid that as best I could.

One of my first steps in this process of exploration was to contact a mentor, who also happened to be one of the Association Ministers in my area. I had relied on his wisdom very often in matters of discernment, and I wanted to process my thoughts and emotions with him and to gain his insights and wisdom. So we set up a time to meet for lunch.

As we waited for our food to arrive, I described to him my state of mind and the need I felt to move to a different setting. He listened intently and patiently as I talked about reaching a plateau, and, while there was always a possibility of finding new vitality where I was, I thought that it was just as possible that this was a sign that the congregation needed fresh pastoral leadership and I needed a change of context. If it turned out to be the latter, I described the type of setting I was looking for, which was similar to the one in which I was confirmed and ultimately nurtured into ministry: a church set in a downtown area of a small town or city, with more of a connection to the surrounding community.

My mentor first affirmed my willingness to test the possibilities of serving in ministry elsewhere and encouraged my desire for my current congregation and I to avoid merely treading water together. Since he also knew what churches were searching or would soon be searching in our area, he named two that seemed to fit the sort of context that I described to him.

The first was a large church in a downtown area, but while set in a small city it was more remote in proximity to other communities and would be more of a challenge for my wife to maintain her professional and educational commitments. There was much to love about this church, but its strain on other parts of my life would be quite notable.

The second was a medium-sized church also in a downtown area, with easy access to several major northeast Ohio cities. It had more substantial resources than where I was and a strong connection to the surrounding community, and my wife would easily be able to continue in what she needed to do for work and school. Most signs seemed to point to this second congregation, but one factor made me wonder: their previous minister had served there for twenty-six years and was still living in the community.

I had good reason to feel hesitant about these factors. When I was born, my pastor father was serving a church in a suburb of Detroit. He had followed a pastorate of significant length, and that was a contributing factor to the issues that caused him to leave after only three years. I did not want to repeat this piece from my family history. I voiced this concern to my mentor, who assured me that the congregation was ready to move into a new beginning. They'd voiced this eagerness to him, and he didn't think that following such a long tenure would be an issue. Trusting that this really was the case, I decided to explore both options.

Just as I'd voiced my concerns about following such a lengthy pastorate to my mentor, I also made sure to ask the church's search committee about it once I began interviewing with them. I asked about the status of their relationship with their former minister and how ready people really did seem to move on. Just as my mentor said, this group assured me that after such a long time of being used to one way of doing things, they wanted to move into the future with a change in direction, one that would diverge from what came before and that would enjoy a new energy.

The more I listened, the more I believed this desire to be genuine. This church's profile and needs continually rose to the top of my mind in my discernment. With every step in the process, it seemed clearer and clearer to me that this would be where the next phase of my vocational life would begin. And sure enough, in November of that year, the congregation voted to extend a call to me to be their next pastor.

On my first official day, I pulled up to the church, filled with excitement for this new partnership. I walked up to the door outside of the offices, which was surrounded by a handful of members, retired men who regularly volunteered once a week to perform maintenance on the building. They were doing something to the lock as I strolled up but stopped to say hello, their own excitement at this time of beginning evident in their greeting.

I walked into my office, set down my bag, and began to acclimate myself to these new surroundings. I figured that I'd spend this time slowly exploring the congregation's rhythms and maybe even reminding myself of the building layout since it had been a while since I'd been inside. It was already Tuesday, which meant I needed to begin thinking about worship and sermon preparation as well.

About an hour into my morning, I heard the secretary's phone ring and a moment later she appeared in the doorway. The patriarch of a member family had just died, and they wanted my predecessor to come back and officiate his funeral.

In just the span of a few minutes, all the assurances that I'd been given over the previous year seemed to evaporate. As often as I'd been told that this church was primed for something new and was ready to move on from what came before, here was the expression of a desire to hang on to that former relationship. And this request quickly presented not only that desire, but a choice of whether or how to indulge it.

Lest the reader think that my hesitation in this case was only about my own ego, the United Church of Christ's ministry resources strongly recommend that a minister, once they depart, give up all pastoral responsibilities to that congregation. This helps a church move on from their previous pastorate so that it has a better chance of establishing a stronger connection to the next one. I wanted to do my part to honor these best practices, recollecting what a failure to do so had done to my family decades earlier. If I said yes in this instance, would more members feel license to ask as well? And if I kept saying yes and they kept asking, how would I ever be able to engage fully in a ministry relationship with them, let alone help them pursue the new beginning for which they'd articulated a hope during the search process?

With all of this in mind, I decided that I had to draw a line in the sand on my very first day. I said that I would be happy to work with the family as the officiant for their loved one's service. With reluctance and some anger, they agreed. What I thought would be a slow time of familiarizing myself with my new surroundings had instead been a difficult moment of setting a boundary.

It also brought a realization that this church was not in the sort of mindset to move forward into the future just yet. It needed more time and guidance to reconcile with the past first. And, whether I expected to or not, I was going to need to be the one to provide it.

INTENTIONAL OR UNINTENTIONAL?

Not every Christian denomination or tradition uses the concept of the interim minister. Many traditions rooted in Methodism, for instance, use an appointment system: bishops assign ministers to a church, evaluate the state of that ministry relationship annually, and then make pastoral changes accordingly. Other traditions and many independent churches use a succession model, in which a candidate from within a church is groomed to take over leadership responsibilities leading up to an impending ministerial departure or retirement.

In denominations such as the United Church of Christ, however, ministers are selected through a process in which the congregation has the final word. In the UCC's system, known as Search and Call, a minister prepares a Ministerial Profile (basically an exhaustive curriculum vitae that includes writing essays and submitting to a background check) and has it sent to churches that have open positions. Likewise, the congregation via an appointed search committee also prepares a profile, which is sent to potential candidates. Ministers and search committees who express interest in one another go through a series of interviews, and the final candidate selected by the committee is voted upon by the entire congregation after a weekend that includes a chance for them to meet their potential new minister and experience their worship leadership.

This type of search process may take at least twelve to twenty-four months, and sometimes longer depending on the circumstances of a particular church's situation. As a result, a congregation is without a settled minister during that in-between time. The original practice often observed in these cases was to have a retired minister step in and "mind the store," providing basic duties like Sunday morning worship and pastoral care.

In the late 1960s, however, a group of researchers began analyzing both the needs and potential of these times between settled ministers. A five-year study conducted by affiliates of the Alban Institute resulted in a paper presented at the Association of Religion and Applied Behavioral Sciences entitled "The Interim Pastor: A Neglected Role in Parish Development." This paper suggested that these in-between times in congregations were quite fertile for congregational self-reflection, so long as the minister serving during those times was equipped with the gifts and knowledge necessary to guide them through it. In 1981, a cross-denominational organization known as the Interim Ministry Network (IMN) spun off from the Alban Institute, established for the purpose of training and networking ministers seeking to serve in this unique role.[1]

Today, the phrase "intentional interim minister" is used to describe ministers who have been specifically trained to handle the tasks entrusted to them as they serve churches while they both make peace with their previous minister's departure and go through the search process to find their next one. Rather than being tasked with merely keeping the pulpit warm until a new minister arrives, these ministers are trained in elements of systems theory to lead a congregation through a time of deliberation about their past and present, as well as preparation for their future. In the best of circumstances, a church will enter their relationship with their new minister with a greater self-awareness and readiness to work together.

Unfortunately, no system or process is perfect. For a variety of reasons, a church may not be so eager to receive the new beginning that a minister's arrival signals. The interim period may not have been long enough, or the process through which the interim minister led them may not have taken root among its members. As a result, a new minister may find themselves having to continue this transitional work in some way.

In 1977, pastor and church consultant Lyle Schaller coined a term to describe ministers who end up in these predicaments. Playing off the term recently established by Alban, he called these clergy "unintentional interim pastors":

> These are the ministers who came to what each understood to be a permanent pastorate, only to find themselves in the role of the transitional pastor serving in a somewhat precarious situation following the end of a distinctive pastorate in that congregation's history . . . before the situation is ready for another permanent pastor. This transitional period between long pastorates or between eras in a congregation's history usually extends from six to twenty-four months, but occasionally it takes three or four or five years to bridge this transitional period. Usually the pastor who serves in this transitional period moves after a period of two or three or four years.[2]

An unintentional interim minister does not expect to end up in this type of situation. They may have some of the same training as intentional interims and may have elected to go through the entire basic interim program offered by the IMN to buttress the education that they received elsewhere. But when a noninterim minister begins a new pastorate, they do so with the understanding that the congregation to which they have been called is ready to embrace the possibilities that this partnership will present.

Instead, the congregation may still need to reconcile with lingering issues from their predecessor's time among them, or they may still be working through a time of conflict that has not yet been resolved. In these instances, such issues take front and center immediately: they are so prominent in the congregational psyche that any other new ministry initiative will feel, and likely be sabotaged by, its effects.

Thus, the unintentional interim is so named because it is a role that the new minister didn't sign up for, but now has no choice but to accept. Their main tasks involve continuing to lead a church through a time of transition that preceded them, and of which their arrival is a point of continuation.

As Schaller observes, most who find themselves serving in unintentional interim roles do not end up lasting very long. Due to the combination of the unexpected nature of their ministry tasks, the prominent presence of conflict, and a tendency to experience burnout, an unintentional interim will usually move on after only a few years. Maybe they were able to help the congregation resolve their enduring time of transition, or maybe that time will also succeed them. Hindsight may provide a clearer conclusion than while these ministers are still serving or shortly after they move on.

TRANSITIONS ARE ALL WE KNOW

As if the transitions internal to a congregation aren't enough, we are in a time of increasing cultural and societal transitions that inevitably have had an impact on the culture of a local church. The causes of a church experiencing instability, uncertainty, or conflict may primarily reside within, but outside factors may also add to the pressure that both minister and congregation feel as they navigate a time of change and all the heightened emotions that accompany it.

In late 2019, news outlets in the United States began sharing stories of a strange new virus that had been detected in Wuhan, China. These reports persisted into the beginning months of 2020, with the virus quickly becoming so widespread across Asia and Europe that countries began instituting lockdowns to help get it under control. One of the enduring images of those earliest months was of entire neighborhoods engaging in singalongs on their balconies as people were stuck in their apartments. Most North American residents watched this with fascination, but also perhaps with anticipation that this disease would eventually reach our shores.

Sure enough, the first case of COVID-19 in the United States was detected on January 21. By February, travel had been restricted and a national health emergency was declared. Most states had declared shutdown measures by mid-March, and businesses, schools, and houses of worship announced that they would be closed until further notice.[3]

Facing questions of how to continue any of their ministries during these shutdowns, many churches quickly pivoted to offering some kind of worship service that next Sunday using their websites or social media. Some pastors broadcast out of their homes, while others set up a camera in their sanctuaries either by themselves or with a skeleton crew of musicians and technicians. As the months of the pandemic dragged on, these online offerings became more streamlined and sophisticated as those with more resources or tech-savvy members figured out how to add graphics, closed captioning, and multiple camera angles. Pastors also adapted their pastoral care practices, making greater use of phone calls and video conferencing to check in with members. Sunday school programs and weekly Bible studies also moved online. Churches also explored and implemented electronic forms of collecting the offering.

As restrictions began to decrease, the question of what to do with this greater emphasis on technology presented itself to ministers and their governing boards. For those willing to seriously engage the issue rather than simply declare its elimination now that they were gathering in person again, churches noted an increase in attendance and accessibility among many who would not typically attend previously. Among other groups, the elderly, disabled, and LGBTQ people were attending services online, whereas previously they hadn't been able to participate due to physical limitations or alienation. If churches wanted to continue including these and other groups, they would not be able to merely do away with this new feature.[4]

The pandemic also hastened cultural trends that previously had been moving much slower. For instance, while churches may be able to celebrate a higher number of attendees and guests on their online platforms, they are also experiencing a sustained dip in in-person attendance. According to Pew Research, 64 percent of churchgoers who would attend in-person before the pandemic had returned to that practice in September 2021. Six months later in March 2022, that number had climbed to 67 percent, suggesting a leveling off to which churches must now adapt.[5]

As if this wasn't enough, larger trends have already indicated a rise in two religious (or perhaps nonreligious) groups. First, the "nones," shorthand for those who check the "no affiliation" box on religious surveys, has climbed to 25 percent of the population as of 2021, with 34 percent of people ages eighteen to twenty-nine identifying themselves as such.[6] The second group, which has only started to catch the interest of religious analysts in recent years, is known as the "dones." These are people who were formerly involved in church life—usually highly committed, in fact—but for various reasons have chosen to step away after so many years of involvement.[7] Those considering themselves "dones" may be included among that one-third who have not returned since pandemic restrictions have eased.

Another awakening particularly among majority white congregations and denominations also took a great step forward around the same time as pandemic lockdowns began. On May 25, 2020, a black man named George Floyd was detained by Minneapolis police. One officer, Derek Chauvin, pressed his knee to Floyd's neck for almost nine minutes, ultimately cutting off air to his lungs and killing him.

Protests calling attention to this act of violence and the larger racial issues that helped cause it were immediate and persisted through the summer. What began years earlier with the deaths of Trayvon Martin and Michael Brown had reached a breaking point. Many who organized and led these protests were pastors, churches, and other faith leaders. It galvanized Christians of all races and ethnicities across the world. This included many white Christians and churches, who seemed to see both their privilege and responsibility anew. In her book *Church Cracked Open*, Episcopal Canon Stephanie Spellers reflects on what transpired among faith communities during those months. She observes the compounding effect that both the COVID-19 pandemic and these protests had together: "I wonder if the cracking of the first pandemic broke us open so that we could see and feel afresh the persistent reality of racism and oppression."[8]

As a result of this renewed awareness of racialized violence in the United States, these protests served as an opportunity for many white churches to begin struggling with their own participation in and response to white supremacy and systemic racism. As Canon Spellers observes, the cracks already produced by the COVID-19 pandemic may have helped make room to perceive the pain and injustice of historical and ongoing racial injustice.

This is a time of tremendous transition for most churches. It is a time when churches have had no choice but to reevaluate their identity and practices in light of numerous changes in their communities and world. These questions may yet be far from settled, and so most ministers may find themselves in the role of an unintentional interim for a time as they guide their congregations through this transitional season. This may not be what people serving in ministry expected to have to deal with prior to 2020, but it is nevertheless what we are faced with addressing now.

SUCCEEDING OURSELVES

My seminary years are receding further and further into the rearview mirror of my life. They were incredibly formative years that I still carry close to my heart, and aspects of that mixture of classroom learning and practical experience continue to inform the way I think about theology, the Bible, and ministry today.

Those years were also a time for which the events of September 11, 2001, set the tone. This event that would alter the lives of so many individuals, our nation, and our world happened a week into my studies. It provided a major piece of the framework with which professors and students alike applied the subject matter of our classes, and even if not the focal point of theological conversation, it nevertheless was a specter hovering over the proceedings. My classmates and I knew that we would be walking into a world that needed a different form of ministry than it did on September 10, even if we were still trying to figure out what that would look like.

Some of the trends I mentioned earlier in this chapter were already happening, even if they weren't yet as pronounced as they are now. By the time I entered my second pastorate—the one in which I would need to take on some explicit unintentional interim tasks—it seemed as if these trends were picking up speed. Whereas I could take more time for slower and more patient congregational education before, the specifics of my new surroundings would also be influenced by the emotions surrounding the end of a longtime pastorate. Some would see this as an opportunity to explore spiritual options elsewhere, others would express the hope for changes not previously thought possible, and still others would decide a change in pastoral relationship would not include them going forward. The combination of wider changes and congregational change would add challenges to this time of ministry both for the church and for me as their pastor.

The events of 2020 would expedite these changes even more, causing more people in every church to reconsider their relationships to their faith communities and to institutional religion in general. As statistics indicate, people who were previously committed to a church are exploring how or whether to continue that commitment in light of all that has happened. Some are reengaging or finding communal acceptance for the first time, while others are moving on to other spiritual opportunities or joining the "dones." The seeds that have contributed to individual decisions may have already been planted, or they may have finally reached fertile soil beginning in March 2020. In any case, the world has changed again, and this Walter Brueggemann quote applies anew for ministers today as it did after 9/11: "The world for which you have been so carefully prepared is being taken away from you by the grace of God."[9]

Those currently serving in ministry may be wondering where exactly the grace of God has been in all that has been happening in recent years. They may be wondering where the grace of God is in shifting attendance numbers and in having to learn new technological skills on short notice. They may wonder where the grace of God is in increased polarization and heightened anxiety among members of their congregations, not to mention of our nation and world. They may wonder how the grace of God may be equipping them to give prophetic voice to injustice and systemic racism. They may wonder if the grace of God, so wonderful and cherished a gospel, may be proclaimed in such uncertain times. And they may wonder whether the grace of God will be enough for them to continue in faithful service at all.

Perhaps we may begin to find the answer to these questions in another set of questions that Lyle Schaller poses in his continued reflections on the role of the unintentional interim:

> However, conceptualizing a pastorate as a series of chapters, rather than measuring it in years, opens the door to another alternative for the unintentional interim pastor. Is this situation one in which I can succeed myself? Can I be the permanent pastor here following myself as the transitional pastor? If the pastor and the members see this transitional period as chapter one of a multichapter pastorate, they may agree that the unintentional interim pastor should follow [themselves] and be the permanent pastor here.[10]

A chapter of ministry that heavily features transition and all of the difficult tasks that accompany it may present challenges related to ministerial discernment and identity. It will signal a world for which we may have been carefully prepared passing away, even being ripped from our grasp by the particular circumstances of the congregation or the larger circumstances of our world. And yet there may also be an opportunity to write an additional chapter, one in which something new begins to take shape between and among the minister and church, in which the unintentional interim succeeds themselves and takes on a different role among the people.

It may also not work out so wonderfully as that. I will certainly not claim any assurance of a positive outcome.

What I will do instead is present some tools and topics for your reflection. They are to help guide you in present and future times of ministry-related transition, to provide grounding as you do your best to navigate through it. If nothing else, they are to remind you that the grace of God is a constant presence in anxious and uncertain times, and it may give you the courage, strength, and inner peace to move through them, whether you're able to succeed yourself or to discern when you have brought a group of God's people as far as you can.

However unintentionally, we are all serving as transitional ministers in one way or another. Let's write this chapter as faithfully as we are able.

JOURNALING PRACTICE

1. Inhale a deep breath through the nose, and exhale through the mouth. Repeat this as many times as necessary to center yourself for the practice.
2. Draw a line down the middle of a page. Give one column the heading "Cultural Transitions," and give the other "Personal Transitions." Under "Cultural Transitions," list all the shifts in the wider culture, including those in your ministry setting, that are foremost on your heart and mind. Under "Personal Transitions," list all the shifts that you are currently experiencing in your own life. This could include health, family, employment, and so on.
3. Take time to ponder each list and notice your internal reactions to each item as you reread them. Which of them makes you anxious, or sad, or

angry, or excited? Are any such reactions new to you, as if you're noticing them for the first time? Note these reactions in your journal.

4. Write about the relationship between these lists, your internal reactions, and your current sense of call to ministry.
5. Repeat the breathing exercise until you feel moved to re-enter your day. Give thanks to God for this time.

2

First Comes Disillusionment

As mentioned in the previous chapter, I am the son of a pastor. Ministry is ingrained into my family heritage several generations back. My great-great-grandfather, Rev. Anders Gustav Nelson, was a minister in the Swedish Mission Covenant Church. "A. G." emigrated to the United States as a missionary in 1871, part of a large wave of Swedish Mission Covenant members to do so. In 1885, many from this group formed the Swedish Evangelical Mission Covenant of America in Chicago, a loose covenant of churches dedicated to pietistic expressions of faith. Committed to do his part in the Swedish Evangelical Mission Covenant, Rev. A. G. Nelson planted and pastored churches around New England and the Midwest. This new movement changed its name to the Evangelical Covenant Church in 1954 and is still in existence today.

Given this family lineage of ministers that endured through my father's eventual ordination and service in the United Church of Christ, during my own studies for the ministry I occasionally encountered the assumption that I was undergoing these preparations because it was my turn to go into the "family business." But I was and still am quick to correct those who think this. I did not go into the ministry *because* my dad was a pastor, but *despite* it.

I have already told one story about a negative experience that my family had while my dad was in his second pastorate. Having followed a long-tenured predecessor, he became the easy target for the congregation's unresolved grief and anxiety related to that transition, which sometimes manifested in incredibly hurtful and vindictive ways. I was far too young at the time to remember anything that happened while we lived there, but I was certainly old enough to witness and even participate in another incident at another church years later.

When I was twelve, we had been living in the parsonage of a church in a rural part of northeast Ohio. This was after spending time at two more churches around Michigan, first in the Upper Peninsula and then close to the Indiana border. My brother had been born during the latter, and, shortly after, we moved further south to this remote part of the state. After such short stints at the previous two stops, I was beginning to settle in at this latest one, enjoying the wide open countryside to ride bikes with friends and a sizable hill down which to sled in the winter.

One afternoon, the phone rang while I was playing in the living room. My dad was out attending to the ministry tasks of the day, while my mom was on the other side of the house preoccupied with household chores. And so, just as I'd been taught, I walked over to the phone and picked up the receiver. The voice on the other end—an older woman who never happened to give her name—asked to speak with my dad. Once again, as taught, I answered that he wasn't home and I offered to take a message to pass along.

She said, "You tell him that if he doesn't change his tactics, he's not going to have a church."

I don't remember anything else that this person said after that, although she did keep talking for a while. I don't even know how long I held the phone up to my ear before my mom came into the room to see what was going on. After seeing the bewildered look on my face, she took the receiver from me, listened herself for a moment, and then hung up.

I went through the rest of the day feeling confused. As a faithful attendee of Sunday School and Vacation Bible School for years whether I wanted to be or not, I kept hearing about this man named Jesus who taught and told stories about love, forgiveness, helping others, and making peace, and about the church being the place where we not only learned about him but were called to follow his teachings. And yet, this person on the other end of the phone had just issued this threat to my family.

My confusion endured that evening as a few trusted members stopped over to sit down with my dad and talk over the implications and possibilities of this phone call. They even called me over at one point to ask me to recall what the person had said, although I'd already forgotten anything after her first declaration. That confusion continued through the next few months, as my parents first pulled me aside pledging to fight what was happening, and then later told me that my dad planned to resign during a congregational meeting. At that point, my confusion turned to anger and sadness as we prepared to move to yet another house and another school system and start our lives over once again.

Years later, I'd begin interviewing with search committees to begin my own career in full-time pastoral ministry. I was by then twenty-five years old, having gone straight from high school to college and then to seminary, a path of education and training that is not nearly as typical or conventional as it once was. During that initial season of search, every interview would eventually get around to the same question: "At such a young age, what experience do you believe you would bring?"

My answer always began with the fact that I come from a family of pastors and other ministry workers. By that point, my mother had become a dedicated and transformational youth group coordinator, so I was now able to cite both sides of my family in such a discussion. But having spent a lifetime in churches, I always shared with those committees that I had been privy to the good, the bad, and the ugly regarding the ways that churches conduct themselves, including how members sometimes treat one another and how they sometimes treat their ministers.

As I was right on the cusp of beginning my own ministerial journey, I was in for years of experiences ahead that would fall into all three categories. And while some of the bad and the ugly would sometimes shock me, none of it would ever really surprise me. I had lost my illusions about the church years earlier after I crossed the living room to pick up the phone.

LOSING OUR ILLUSIONS

When one hears the term "disillusionment," it may conjure a certain set of connotations. When one says that they are disillusioned about something, it usually comes with feelings that we perceive as negative. We tend to associate disillusionment with despair, disappointment, frustration, and hopelessness. And perhaps the word has earned these associations, because disillusionment frequently causes such reactions in the person who experiences it.

However, removed from value judgements that we may place upon it, to become disillusioned is simply to lose an illusion that one has about something. It is the passing away of a false idea that we have in order to see something in more realistic terms.

Think, for instance, about the development of a relationship. When you first meet someone, you may each try to highlight your best qualities to make a positive impression, while also keeping certain personality traits or opinions at bay. You may also guard parts of yourself that you reserve for those for whom you have greater trust, and that you don't believe should be shared so early with those whom you don't know as well. Of course, the other person is also likely doing this for similar reasons.

As this new relationship progresses and deepens, and each person involved experiences greater relaxation and trust, those other personality traits, opinions, and guarded history may begin to appear. As this unfolds, each person will begin to lose the illusions that they had during those first more surface-level interactions. You may have had a certain impression of the other person based on those earlier times, and they of you. But as you each reveal more of yourselves to the other, pieces of those impressions begin to fall away, and you each gain greater clarity.

This may result in a better understanding of the other's true self. Each revelation will also bring a series of reactions, including surprise, joy, greater impressiveness, and deeper love. These reactions may also include doubt, disappointment, hesitation, or even fear. Either way, such clarity can be beneficial, because it helps us see whether this relationship has potential to continue or would be better off coming to an end.

In this example, disillusionment is not necessarily problematic. Rather, it merely brings a more realistic idea of what is currently happening or could happen in the future. It helps us see people, places, groups, events, and institutions more as they actually are, rather than as we think they are. True enough, that may bring negative emotions about the work ahead of us or the limitations on that work. But losing our illusions will help clarify what the work really is.

The theologian Reinhold Neibuhr was a fan of disillusionment when it came to clergy and church leadership:

> A spiritual leader who has too many illusions is useless. One who has lost [their] illusions about [humanity] and retains [their] illusions about [themselves] is insufferable. Let the process of disillusionment continue until the self is included. At that point, of course, only religion can save from the enervation of despair. But it is at that point that true religion is born.[1]

Neibuhr wrote this reflection after hearing an itinerant preacher position themselves as a prophet, propping themselves up as the truth-teller and the room's sole bearer of compassion for the state of the world. This no doubt prompted Neibuhr's words about insufferability. This person had an illusion about self set over and against (and above) the audience, which propped up a barrier between the preacher and those listening.

Today's spiritual leaders are not exempt from this and many other illusions about themselves. Those who serve in ministry may harbor illusions about their theological knowledge, liturgical purity, academic credentials, or ministerial acumen. This can lead to a detachment from and even resentment of the people to whom they are trying to minister. Meanwhile such leaders may also miss out on the wealth of experience and wisdom upon which they may draw to minister more effectively in partnership together.

More privileged spiritual leaders who have good intentions about speaking up for or taking action on behalf of the oppressed and less fortunate may be doing so ignorant of how their own sexism, racism, homophobia, transphobia, and ableism are nevertheless influencing their activity or lack of activity on such matters. In these cases, the work of disillusionment is always before such leaders, and they will benefit from a stance of listening and centering voices and experiences that differ from their own. This will help the minister gain greater clarity about themselves and the appropriate nature of their work in relation to those whom they wish to help.

In any new ministry venture, disillusionment will be one of the first experiences that helps a minister understand the true nature of the ministry partnership, beginning as early as the first interview or the first official day. The relationship between a minister and congregation, like any relationship, may begin on the surface. The minister will have certain hopes and impressions based on what they already know about the congregation, and the congregation likewise will have their own hopes and ideas based on their limited interactions with the new minister before this date.

As the relationship unfolds further, however, each will gain greater understanding of the other's preferences, habits, routines, leanings, and even a few potential dealbreakers. The reality may not match each party's hopes and impressions. Maybe the new minister seems too similar to or too different from the last. Maybe the new congregation isn't as daring or progressive as they previously let on.

The loss of these illusions may bring negative reactions. Among them may be a feeling of loss that things going forward will not be what they have been in the past. I discuss this more in the next chapter.

Other negative reactions include disappointment or frustration. A church or minister may have high hopes for a new initiative, only for it to not catch on with as much energy as expected. A minister may harbor a vision of a church willing to follow them into greater involvement with justice and outreach activities, only to face more resistance or apathy. A church may expect a minister to galvanize a new wave of involvement from the surrounding community only to find that more work needs to be done for that to happen. Each of these losses of an illusion may bring disappointment, with one or both sides questioning what will be possible together. They may experience a decline in interest, a hesitancy to work up the energy to try something else, or an increased wariness of the ministry partnership. If the lost illusion or the resultant negative feelings are big enough, a church or minister may not be as enthusiastic for the next initiative, or they may not even want to organize it to begin with.

Negative reactions to disillusionment are natural, and the scope will vary case by case. It may take time and intention for both minister and congregation to work through them. However, once these illusions have begun to fall away, a more honest relationship also will be possible.

ADJUSTING EXPECTATIONS

Not only do ministers struggle with the illusions and expectations they have of themselves, they also frequently encounter those of their church members. Whether it's someone attending for the first time or a longtime member, each may expect different things out of the church they attend. Such expectations may vary by generation, life stage, personal development, and personal preferences.

The oldest among us—those who fall in the Baby Boomer generation and older—may still be used to the church as a major source of socialization and a place where friend groups gather. As a result, they may expect fellowship activities such as dinners and game groups, like they've always known churches and communities to provide.

Families may wish for the church to be part of their children's development, both morally and socially (some opportunities to drop them off for a while so parents can run errands or go out for a kid-free evening wouldn't hurt, either). As a result, families may expect groups or events for their children, either simply to get them involved in something, to help teach them about faith, or even just because it will look good on a college application.

Youth may expect something worth engaging in—not necessarily to be entertained, but to be engaged: to be taken seriously, to have room to ask questions, and to be validated for who they are. In this stage of their lives, a space to affirm who they are discovering themselves to be while teaching them about the full possibilities of following Jesus and being part of the church will be important. Treating them as full members of the church now rather than when older generations are ready to cede power will be important, too.

A church's surrounding community may have hopes and expectations for it as well. If the church has a history as a hub for gathering or outreach, community members may naturally gravitate toward it as a space to host neighborhood events or as a place for those in need to receive assistance.

There are other programmatic things that members may expect: opportunities to learn more about the Bible or discipleship, engaging worship, a chance to be in community or to be welcomed, preaching that relates the Bible to everyday life (variations on this phrase have appeared on every church profile I've ever read while in Search and Call).

Church members may expect their churches to do or be certain things *for them*. None of the forementioned things are bad or not worthwhile, and there's no reason for churches not to do their best within their means to encourage and organize education, mission, worship, and fellowship for members and nonmembers alike. But they do all happen to be things that we want to be provided for our benefit in some way.

These expectations need to include what we expect to contribute to a community: how we help organize fellowship, how we encourage or engage our children and youth, how we help ease the needs of others, what kind of energy we bring to worship, how we welcome others.

When a church—ours or another—somehow fails to live up to these expectations, that may be a source of disillusionment for us. But the causes for this failure are becoming more complex and common, some of which were mentioned in the previous chapter.

As older generations are not as able to attend church activities, opportunities for traditional fellowship may diminish since they are usually the ones who provide the most energy for them. As illusions about the church as a major social gathering space fall away, churches will be faced with a changed view of how and why members gather.

As families have increased demands on their time from school and extracurricular activities, their view of the church as a primary space for learning and development may shift. Along with this, the illusion of a church needing to provide activities for children and youth in the same way they have for the past half century or more may fall away, leaving room for other possibilities.

As youth may or may not face the same pressure to be part of a faith community, the illusion of church activities needing to be entertaining in order for youth to attend may be passing away in favor of making space for genuine connection.

As neighborhoods around churches change, members move further away, and community needs become more prominent, a church that relies on their members to drive the energy of activities and is used to the walls of their building holding themselves in and the wider community out may need to lose that illusion of the church as a fortress in favor of something more permeable and outwardly engaging.

The loss of these illusions may initially bring concern, sadness, anxiety, and a pining for what used to be. As mentioned, disillusionment often causes these sorts of reactions. Our current pandemic-informed season has already done so, and these reactions may continue to dwell within individuals and congregations as they do their best to adjust and respond. A frequent reaction in many settings is to place increased blame and pressure on the minister to right the ship. Members may demand that their minister return them to a time of former prosperity, or even just to a better reality that they enjoyed a few short years prior. At its heart, this is an expression of grief, and yet it also can be quite unfair and damaging.

The loss of these illusions will bring an opportunity to reimagine how a church may approach the same activities in a new way or develop new ministries that meet the needs that these changes signal. This may require much internal work for the minister to remain centered, patient, and calm as members experience these losses before gently pivoting them into a time of imagining what to do next.

Disillusionment can be hard when it first presents itself. But ministers and churches able to recognize, process, and adapt when it happens have a better chance to enjoy a longer, healthier, deeper, and more meaningful relationship.

THE POSITIVE SIDE OF DISILLUSIONMENT

The years that followed my experience with my father's anonymous caller eventually brought a renewed confidence in what the church can be. My family moved to another community, and I started the confirmation program in the church that we began attending. This was followed by regular involvement in youth group and mission trips, helping lead worship, and engaging in other activities. I continued to carry the altered perception that the earlier experience presented, but I was also able to appreciate what a church can be when it acts in healthy and supportive ways. This was the "good" of the good, bad, and ugly that I'd later talk about with pastor search committees.

By the time I'd begun in my second pastorate, I'd seen even more of the good, bad, and ugly of individual Christians' and churches' behavior, and I'd heard more about my dad's past experience in his pastorate that had succeeded a long previous tenure. These stories and experiences of disillusionment helped prepare me for that first morning when I fully realized that my own time following a longer pastorate would provide more challenges and take more time than indicated to me up to that point.

For the church's part, they likely also experienced the loss of illusions. Primary among these was the realization that their previous pastor really wasn't their pastor any longer. Some would seek ways to get around this when important milestone moments arose in their lives. Other reactions would include a comparing and contrasting of ministry styles, including worship leadership, pastoral care, administration, and even the way I organized my office. I was not what they were used to, and I may not have been who they expected, so they were losing illusions about this new pastoral relationship as well.

However, our mutual loss of illusions was also beneficial, even if we could not always see it. We eventually came to a place in the ministry partnership where we each were able to view one another as we truly were. As a result, we gained a greater ability to keep things in proper perspective. Both churches and ministers are human and are bound to be disappointing, frustrating, and even hurtful. Realizing this will bring a better perception through which one may be more accepting of flaws, mistakes, and failures.

Another benefit of disillusionment is the potential for adaptation. Through the loss of an illusion, a church or minister will experience one less possibility for the future of the ministry partnership. Such a realization may also present additional ideas and possibilities for the partnership not previously considered, in part because one or both parties wanted their illusions of the other to prevail. Once it becomes clear that they won't, there comes an opportunity, or even permission, to adapt to who the other truly is and what may be possible instead.

Finally, another benefit of disillusionment for ministers and congregations together is the doing away with the glamorization of the other. This may at first blush seem like a bad thing, but it helps both sides of the relationship put away their ideals. Pastor and author Eugene Peterson put it like this:

> Anyone who glamorizes congregations does a grave disservice to pastors. We hear tales of glitzy, enthusiastic churches and wonder what in the world we are doing wrong that our people don't turn out that way under our preaching. On close examination, though, it turns out that there are no wonderful congregations. Hang around long enough and sure enough there are gossips who won't shut up, furnaces that malfunction, sermons that misfire, disciples who quit, choirs that go flat—and worse. Every congregation is a congregation of sinners. As if that weren't bad enough, they all have sinners for pastors.[2]

This doing away with glamorization of the self will, as Niebuhr suggests, make us less insufferable.

Clinging to our illusions does a disservice to everyone involved. It sabotages the ministry relationship by insisting that someone else take on an identity that is not theirs for our satisfaction. And it keeps us both from seeing and from appreciating the reality of the imperfect yet no-less-beloved children of God with whom we are called into ministry together.

Losing our illusions about ourselves will help keep us off any pedestal on which we may wish to place ourselves. Losing our illusions of the other may cause us to be disappointed or frustrated that someone else isn't living up to them. But in the long run, it will also keep us from placing them on a pedestal as well, let alone becoming angry that they won't stay up there where we want them. When we experience disillusionment, that's when the real work of ministry may begin.

JOURNALING PRACTICE

1. Inhale a deep breath through the nose, and exhale through the mouth. Repeat this as many times as necessary to center yourself for the practice.
2. Think and write about some past moments that caused you to lose an illusion about ministry, about the ministry setting you were serving at the time, or about yourself. Note how you reacted to this loss of illusion when it happened, as well as its ongoing effect for you now. Does a past moment of disillusionment still live in you, for better or worse?

3. What disillusionment have you experienced in recent times of transition? Note both those that you have been grieving, and those that have led to growth, change, or new learning.
4. Write to a past version of yourself before one such illusion was lost. Offer them reassurance, guidance, and news of what you eventually learned. Be gentle with them as you do so.
5. Repeat the breathing exercise until you feel moved to reenter your day. Give thanks to God for this time.

3

The Pit of Negative Expectations

About three months into my time at my new pastorate, we held my installation service. For those unfamiliar with such a service, this is a special time of worship set aside for the celebration of the new ministry relationship, as well as its formalization through liturgy and the bestowing of a certificate officially recognizing the minister's call to that setting.

I'd been planning the service at least a few weeks in advance. I scheduled it for Pentecost Sunday, so the theme and imagery of the Spirit's call would be omnipresent already. At the urging of my Association Minister, I held it during our morning service rather than planning for a separate one in the afternoon, so that as many members of the church as possible could be there. However, given that installation services also involve covenanting with other UCC churches to serve alongside them, I needed to reach out to invite people from the wider church to attend as well.

Having had the advantage of being in the same Association that ordained me, I was privileged to have many connections in the area from which to pull. My parents attended, and my mom—the youth director at my hometown church—led the children's time, which included sharing many pictures of me growing up, to everyone's delight. I invited a musician I knew to play special music. A friend and colleague from the UCC national setting came to preach, and the Association Associate Minister—a beloved mentor—led the installation liturgy. During the offering, I debuted an original song about how each new place you reside can eventually become home. Sure enough, members of other area UCC congregations attended to be part of the new covenant we were making. And in further recognition of this new communal partnership, we shared in the sacrament of communion.

I wish that I could say that all of this went smoothly, and that there was never a spirit of anxiety or chaos to the morning. However, in true Pentecost fashion, there was enough uncertainty to the proceedings to keep everyone on their toes throughout. First, the Cleveland Marathon was happening the same morning, so my friend who was going to preach had a bit of a struggle getting from her home in that area down to the church in time for the service. I can still picture her hurrying down the hallway toward the sanctuary just as the prelude began. Next, I was so nervous during my song that I ended up warbling through it: the sound technician gave me a recording of it after, and I can't bring myself to listen to it. And finally, any little happening that I didn't think was going as well as I thought for such a moment—any slight lull, any noticed bulletin typo, the fact that the service seemed to be running too long and imagining how people were reacting to that—caused my nerves to fray just a little bit more.

It could have been that nobody else noticed these sorts of imperfections in the moment the way that I did, and, if they did, they may well not have cared. Maybe if people rewatched the service later they'd be able to see them more clearly, and again, some may have reacted with a desire to fix them (like me), while others could more easily brush them aside with a comment about it all being in the past now.

So many years after the fact, I can now count myself as part of the latter group. Such imperfections were unfixable in the moment, and now they've become a good story.

In the moment, however, such instances may bring a feeling of urgency: a desire to get it right, as if all future moments are dependent upon how well this present one goes. Such an urgency comes with a desire for the most perfect and most meaningful moment that it can possibly be, in pursuit of greater affirmation and assurance that what is happening now is a sign that what one is doing is right and good. And conversely, the more imperfections appear to the eyes of the planner or participant, the less meaning, affirmation, and assurance one may feel.

THE PIT OF NEGATIVE EXPECTATIONS

As explored in the previous chapter, disillusionment can inspire a variety of responses. When viewed positively, the loss of an illusion can be approached as a time of learning and recalibration of expectations of the possibilities for ministry in a particular setting. When viewed negatively, however, it may cause one to become disappointed and discouraged. If enough disappointment and discouragement accumulates, it can affect one's overall approach to ministry, and may even lead to a time of discernment or burnout (this will be explored in depth in chapter 9).

University of Michigan sports blogger Brian Cook coined a term for when an increase in discouragement ends up having a lasting effect on one's outlook. If, as in his line of work, those who root for a specific sports team experience a sustained amount of bad play and hopes dashed, a fan may fall into what he calls the "Black Pit of Negative Expectations." In essence, they reach a point where they expect to be let down by their team, no matter what happens on the field. This includes even positive developments: if your team scores, you may not even be able to celebrate it because you're already waiting for the other shoe to drop. Being in the Pit of Negative Expectations means that you can't be happy for the good things that happen, because you're already waiting for the next bad thing to happen that will not only negate but eclipse the good.[1]

This Pit of Negative Expectations can take a toll on a ministry partnership, whether the minister, the ministry setting, or both feel stuck down inside it. While it begins as an outlook and a mindset, it inevitably will affect behavior as well. Here is a nonexhaustive list of what "the Pit" can include, as well as how it may manifest in ministry.

Pessimism—This is essentially a synonym for this way of viewing one's ministry. It features the expectation that either things will go wrong, or not enough things will go right, resulting in a ministry initiative that will end in failure.

Decreased effort—If your expectations for ministry are negative, it will affect the amount of effort that you will put into it. Concluding that little to no positive outcome will result from an act of ministry will lead to putting less effort into it to begin with, increasing the likelihood of a self-fulfilling prophecy.

Fear—Approaching ministry with negative expectations can cause a turning inward, a shrinking away from trying anything new for fear that you will feel disappointment once again. Fear will cause ministers and churches to focus on the ways things may go wrong, rather than on exciting and hopeful possibilities.

Avoidance—A natural outcome of fear will be a tendency to avoid experiences that one perceives could result in disappointment or feelings of failure. This will cause a further shrinking away from exploring any kind of new initiatives.

Preoccupation with mistakes—As mentioned, the Pit of Negative Expectations heavily involves a preoccupation with the negative, no matter how much positive has also happened. As was the case with certain parts of my installation service, at times I could only see the mistakes at the expense of the larger experience. This can cause an unfair judgment of the situation.

Overthinking—As several of these characteristics already show, a ministry partnership mired in negative expectations can become stuck in both thinking too much about past failures, mistakes, and losses of illusions, as well as becoming too focused on ways new opportunities could go wrong. One or both partners could spend so much time thinking about something that nothing is ever accomplished, or if it is, it is done much more slowly than necessary.

Scarcity—A scarcity mindset will view everything in terms of not being enough. If an event has fewer attendees than expected, ministers and churches will evaluate it as "only" having that many people rather than celebrating the positive difference it made for those who did attend. For new possible activities, one or both may view resources in terms of a need for more, possibly leading to acting with decreased effort or avoidance of going through with anything at all.

Self-isolation—There is likely to come a point where those who speak of negative expectations for themselves or for ministry possibilities will become more alienated from others. Those who are trying to focus on positive goals or celebrate positive outcomes will become more and more frustrated by pessimism or criticism that adds little by way of actual solutions.

One may naturally wonder how to begin climbing out of the Pit of Negative Expectations. If the listed characteristics are both unhealthy and unhelpful ways to view our sense of self and to approach our work, how might we move toward something more positive for ourselves and for the ministry partnership?

The first tendency we may have may be to take the preceding list and consider the opposite. If a mindset of negative expectations features pessimism, then we need to lean into optimism. If this mindset comes with fear, then we need to be more courageous, and so on. However, this approach risks moving to a space of toxic positivity, where the root causes that led us into "the Pit" to begin with go unaddressed. Trying to will oneself to be more optimistic or to stop overthinking may work for a short while in an artificial way, but in the longer term it will be easy to slip back into familiar thought patterns and habits.

This second, much shorter list of ways to address the Pit of Negative Expectations is less about opposites and more about awareness. Cultivating a different view and approach will involve becoming conscious of ourselves and others in alternative ways. Again, while not exhaustive, these are a few of the ways in which that may begin to happen.

Presence—One of my martial arts instructors often likes to say, "it's in the past." Did you make a mistake? It's in the past. Did something not go as well as you hoped? It's in the past. The moment in which something happened that left you dissatisfied is now a memory. In the meantime, you've been presented with a new moment, and dwelling on that memory will distract you from meeting the new moment as fully as you are able.

Being present means tending to the circumstances of now, as well as bringing your gifts to those circumstances as completely as you can. Doing so involves sensing what is happening around you: what do you see, hear, and notice from others, as well as from within yourself? How are you equipped to respond, or how can you partner with others to respond? Dwelling on a former moment does not allow us to do this work of noticing as well as we could otherwise. The call of each new ministry moment is to let the past be past, and to become more in the present.

Activity—While I promised not to provide mere opposites of the previous list, this will be the one exception. While thinking and planning are essential steps in many areas of ministry, there does come a point where they can also be used as stall tactics: excuses to avoid taking action. As ministry is an art rather than a science, we will not be able to account for every potential outcome, and attempts to the contrary will diminish energy over time. Furthermore, becoming mired in the thinking phase—overthinking—can be done to the neglect of a pressing need that will continue to go unaddressed the longer one stalls on making a decision.

There will come a moment when taking action despite worry, fear, hesitancy, and a preference for avoidance will be necessary. The new dynamic that arises as a result of action will bring its own opportunities and challenges, but you won't know what those are until you move the situation forward no matter how slightly, with real action.

Trust—A common element of negative expectations and many of the resultant reactions in the previous list is a lack of trust. You may fail to trust in yourself to meet the moment as perfectly as you feel you're expected to. You may not trust your own knowledge and ability, despite years of learning, training, experience, and study to the contrary. You may fail to trust in others, as you feel the need to take on more responsibility than you truly need to carry despite the presence of other knowledgeable and capable partners in the work. Finally, you may fail to trust that things aren't as bad as you think they are, despite such knowledgeable and capable people giving assurances otherwise.

As with moving from thinking to activity, trust involves giving up a certain amount of control so that a situation can move forward. It involves relying more on the thoughts, opinions, and skills of those with whom you are partnering in ministry. It involves the voices of colleagues and others outside the situation who can provide a different view and help you consider different perspectives, including those that assure you that there are more positive qualities present than what you are able to see.

Listening—Related to trust, listening to those around you can help you temper your negative expectations. Allowing the voices of those who love you, believe in you, and support you to permeate the high walls of "the Pit" can assist you in climbing out of it. These voices are from individuals who know what you are capable of and wish for your success, including trusted church members, fellow clergy, mentors, and others. And trusting these voices involves not only hearing what they say, but receiving it as the gift of encouragement that it is meant to be. Entrusting others with your concerns is a topic we'll explore more when we discuss the Web of the Work in chapter 6.

The Pit of Negative Expectations is not the healthiest or most helpful internal space from which to practice ministry. Recognizing that you are stuck down in it is the first task. Climbing out of it will take some time and effort, but it will be worthwhile and necessary if one wishes to continue doing faithful and effective ministry.

THE ADVANTAGES OF URGENCY

The Pit of Negative Expectations is a space dominated by despair and a strong temptation to give up. It traps us in a state of mind where we find hope difficult to hold for very long. It keeps us believing that nothing can ever change or improve, which in turn will keep us from attempting to take action. In "the Pit," it is easy to become numb and complacent.

The opposite, and thus a strong set of footholds and handholds for climbing out of "the Pit," is a sense of urgency. Urgency brings a desire to do anything but sit and wallow. Instead, it wants to move, explore, plan, and take action. The Apostle Paul shows us how urgency can be beneficial for faith communities.

The letters of Paul included in the New Testament have been used over the centuries to construct entire theological movements handed down from generation to generation. His words have been given transcendent meaning, elevated to a status of authority used to affirm the faithful and condemn the unfaithful: to uphold orthodoxy and condemn heresy. The magnitude with which the words he wrote two thousand years ago have affected the world is difficult to quantify and imagine.

Given all of this, it is sometimes easy to forget that originally these were letters written from a trusted leader to faith communities struggling with questions about how best to live together. So much of what he wrote was meant less to be recognized as eternal truth forever after, and more because particular people were wondering who could be included in this new Jesus-based movement, how best to serve others, what to eat, and how to worship. Much like churches in our contemporary transitional times, the communities to which Paul was writing were just trying to figure some things out, and he was doing his best to advise them.

Take the believers in Corinth as an example. They seemed to be one of the more divided communities to which Paul wrote, as he argued with them about a variety of topics related to inclusion, dietary restrictions, what the concept of grace permitted, and resurrection, among so many others that we could name. He would handle each of their concerns in turn, often peppering his responses with what he knew best about both the Jewish and Greek worlds that he straddled.

In 1 Corinthians 7, Paul addresses a series of concerns about marriage, sexual ethics, circumcision, and slavery. He tackles each of these in quick succession over the span of forty verses. Among other things, he advises married couples to solve their issues quickly and by mutual agreement; unmarried couples to do what they feel they need to do to maintain control of their bodies; the community as a whole not to worry whether someone is circumcised or not; and, in an unsatisfactory, privileged, and harm-reinforcing reply, he tells slaves to relish their spiritual freedom in Christ even if they are not physically free.

In part, this series of responses is informed by Paul's belief that Christ's return was imminent. This series of issues was important for the present social and moral health of the community, but there was also a certain urgency in everything Paul wrote due to his expectation that Jesus would be coming back shortly to reform the world.[2]

This is most clear in verses 29–13:

> I mean, brothers and sisters, the appointed time has grown short; from now on, let even those who have wives be as though they had none, and those who mourn as though they were not mourning, and those who rejoice as though they were not rejoicing, and those who buy as though they had no possessions, and those who deal with the world as though they had no dealings with it. For the present form of this world is passing away (1 Cor. 7:29–31, NRSV).

The time has grown short, Paul says. Marriage, grief, joy, and business are among the myriad of issues that may be relevant and important now, but "the present form of this world is passing away." In a short while, all of this will change. Details about these things will become less critical to sort out. What will remain most important, however, will be to focus on God's purposes and will for each person. Paul wishes for the people of Corinth, as well as the others with whom he is in relationship, to have a sense of urgency about the state of the world and about their obedience to God. Even if we don't get all the details about life right, the details about faithfulness to God matter more, anyway.

Two thousand years later, we're still waiting for God's radical cleanup of the world. Given our current circumstances, some may be hoping as hard as they ever have that it happens soon. Regardless, church practice and thinking has changed over the centuries: the sense of urgency with which Paul operated and which he encouraged for Corinth and others is not as infused in our practices as it once was. Since Paul's time, the church has become a dominant and powerful force in the world, at times enacting charity and justice and at other times reinforcing oppression and violence.

The mainline Protestant church in the United States has had to wrestle with this lack of urgency in its own way. On the one hand, a lack of urgency has allowed us to focus on the here and now, including helping the poor and the downtrodden. We have been given the gift of enough time to attempt to understand how the realm of God is breaking into the world and how individuals can embrace it for themselves.

And yet a lack of urgency can also lead to complacency. It can lull people, churches, and entire Christian movements into a mindset that there will always be more time, and tomorrow will always arrive. As cultural shifts after World War II brought a time of great involvement in a variety of social and civic organizations, churches benefitted alongside many other institutions and enjoyed a time of great prosperity. But the positive effects of these shifts eventually began to wane and other shifts took their place, among them a greater suspicion of formal religious involvement and a wider variety of social and personal activities outside of these longstanding organizations. In response, some movements regained a sense of urgency and adapted, while others did not. Tomorrow would still arrive, the latter would say to themselves, and we will still be here just like always.

In the past decade or so, we have entered a season in which urgency has become front and center for everyone. When the pandemic shutdowns began, ministers and churches had to pivot quickly, doing their imperfect best in a very short amount of time. At first, the minute details mattered less so long as they were able to continue ministering to people in some way. They would have to tweak these new practices as they learned what worked better, learning as they went, just as Paul's communities did. And they constantly would have to deal with occasional slips into the Pit of Negative Expectations as they wondered if anything would ever seem "normal" again. Even after the regulations lifted, "normal" has not seemed to return, and churches are still faced with an urgency they are trying to figure out how to address.

Paul's communities had some advantage with a greater sense of urgency. With urgency comes an increase in passion and energy. There comes a drive to be faithful, and to loosen one's grip on the details that might not be perfect but also don't need to be. There comes a realization that material goods and temporary desires and distractions aren't as important as the continued inbreaking of God's realm and of our own participation in it.

For Paul's churches, there was only the present moment and what they could do to encourage one another to be faithful disciples. Paul didn't want them to take their situation for granted. Rather, he even seemed to hope that a sense of urgency would prevent such a thing from happening.

While today's churches may still choose complacency, it will come with a cost that is becoming steeper every day. The hastening trends of our current times come with an increased demand for a mindful and purposeful response, the alternative being continued diminishment of engagement and resources from both members and the surrounding community. A church that chooses complacency may continue to hope for longevity but does so without a sense of direction of how that will be accomplished.

Longevity must be differentiated from complacency. The former is an *intention* to be around for a long time, while the latter is an *assumption* that one will be around for a long while. Longevity still has a sense of urgency to it, even if that urgency may be expressed in a more thoughtful, planned, structured way. It still asks questions about outreach, relevance, and how it may make a difference in today's world. Churches committed to longevity, and its partner urgency, embrace the strange decisions thrust upon them by moments of crisis or uncertainty and do their best to continue ministry even if the details aren't perfect. A complacent church does so begrudgingly at best, but easily succumbs to the pessimism, avoidance, fear, and scarcity of "the Pit."

The church in every moment is faced with the choice between longevity/urgency and complacency. It can attempt to stick with the approach that it will eventually get to ministry at some undefined point in the future, which won't do much for its effectiveness or relevance. Or it can choose a more urgent approach.

An urgent approach will look at crises such as racist, homophobic, and transphobic violence and ask how best to resist them. It will see once vital ministries falling by the wayside due to lack of interest or energy and ask what new initiatives may capture that interest and energy now. It prioritizes ministry and mission that will make a difference rather than minutiae that serve as distractions. It sees possibilities and empowers laypeople to organize around them rather than relying on ministry staff to initiate.

Transitional times such as our current circumstances have brought a sense of urgency that many churches have not experienced for a long while. The most effective solutions for addressing the needs of our local communities have come with many unknown variables, and the imperfections of our responses have at times been so blatant that the pull to focus on them has been strong. To give in to that pull is to begin the descent into the Pit of Negative Expectations, which will trap ministers and churches alike in a cycle of lower effort and disappointing results. This may especially be the case for those who had chosen complacency for so long.

As with Paul, the right mix of longevity and urgency could yet reveal the path ahead, however imperfect it will be.

JOURNALING PRACTICE

1. Inhale a deep breath through the nose, and exhale through the mouth. Repeat this as many times as necessary to center yourself for the practice.
2. Return to the list of indications that you could be in the Pit of Negative Expectations. Choose those from the list that seem to currently resonate with you the most, and write about their current effect on your thinking, behavior, and ministry. Add others that are not listed and write about them as well.
3. Move to the list of ways to remove yourself from "the Pit." Choose the characteristics to which you feel most drawn and reflect on why. Write down one thing you can do in the next week that will help you pursue each item that you have chosen.
4. Reflect on and write about the presence of urgency and complacency in your ministry, whether interior or exterior. How are you currently finding each helpful and harmful in your work? How might what you wrote about under item 3 address these as well?
5. Repeat the breathing exercise until you feel moved to reenter your day. Give thanks to God for this time.

Seasonal Grief

I read a lot of articles about the decline of the church. The fact that you are reading this book signals that perhaps you have as well. I have lost count of how many words I have read about the future of American Christianity over the years. Numbers are down all over the place. Churches are closing, denominations shrinking, institutions dwindling.

Of course, everyone has their own theory, their own single root factor, to explain why things are progressing the way that they are. People don't gather in formal groups the way they used to. Religious pluralism and an appreciation for multiple viewpoints has been on the rise. Many are more interested in being "spiritual but not religious," "none," or "done." It's the fault of this or that generation. People have more options for things to do on Sunday mornings and would rather do any of them. The church has strayed from the One True Faith as defined by the person who wrote the piece. These are some of the most common explanations I've read in recent times.

Despite their dire subject matter, a fair number of these analyses do tend to have a hopeful tone to them. The decline of the church as an institution is good news, many of them say, because it means we can finally get back to really being the church. No more Constantinian comfort and privilege keeping us from truly following Jesus and helping others! We're entering an exciting and bold new day where the old paradigms are finally passing away and something wonderful and more authentic will take its place. These articles celebrate what is happening, because it means an overdue shedding of heavy baggage in favor of something lighter, nimbler, and more in tune with the rest of the culture.

The national headquarters of my denomination, the United Church of Christ, recently moved from one location to another in downtown Cleveland. In the former space, the UCC owned the entire building, whereas now it rents a floor in a building owned by someone else. When it was in its previous space, I only ever visited a handful of times despite living relatively close by. Whenever I did have the chance to visit, I always made it a point to stop in to see the sanctuary space on the ground floor known as the Amistad Chapel.

The chapel was a beautiful space, very modern yet tasteful. The communion table rested in the center, a deliberate focal point and embodied theological statement about sacred community. It housed two organs, one a larger Hammond and the other a more modest Bedient. Distributed around the room were artwork, candles, and hymnals, among other sacred artifacts and worship aids. When a team within the national setting announced its plans to place the building on the market and seek a smaller office footprint, I and many others across the denomination wondered about what would happen to the chapel. I'd think about its original purpose of being a sacred place in the middle of a bustling downtown area, and about the possibility of its no longer being there.

One may rightfully argue that the sidewalk outside can be just as sacred, just as infused with God's presence as the polished room that overlooks it. Nevertheless, those concerned for the chapel naturally wondered where the organs, paintings, worship books, and all the rest would end up if and when the national setting changed its address. Where would everything go? Would these pieces help bless others, helping to remind them of God's presence in their lives?

People ask these same sorts of questions whenever a church closes. That organ that led our singing for a hundred years, that sanctuary in which generations were baptized, married, and commended to God, those classrooms in which questions were asked, that office where pastors provided counsel . . . all now gone. Maybe the building will be razed for condominiums or given to a new congregation or just sit dormant until it collapses, an empty reminder of times past.

Church members ask this about situations with lower stakes as well. If our choir, now dwindled to a half dozen tired people, disbands, what will happen to the state of our music ministry? If a long-established Bible study group stops meeting, what will happen to our faith formation opportunities? When a beloved pastor leaves, will the next one keep doing the things we liked about the last one?

We're allowed to grieve the inevitable changes that happen in a congregation's life. In fact, many will need to. We are certainly called into a new future as disciples and as faith communities, but, as with any type of loss, many will not be able simply to barrel forward in joy and thanksgiving. There are lingering emotions that we must be allowed to recognize and that we should affirm in one another. We can't be what we were, but we can be sad, and admit our sadness, before moving into what God wants us to do next.

EXCITEMENT AND SADNESS

A few years into my time in my unintentional interim pastorate, my relationship with the congregation began to turn a corner. I began "succeeding myself" as the settled minister, to use Lyle Schaller's phrase again.

Around this same time, several younger families and individuals approached me with an interest in introducing more modern elements to our worship service.[1] Such a sentiment had been expressed during my search process, and part of the search committee's interest in me as a candidate stemmed from my blending such elements into the service at my previous church. The search committee and others saw this as part of the new beginning for which they were hoping after the departure of their previous long-tenured minister. This group of members had longed for such a style of worship for years, but for various reasons could not see it happening before my arrival.

I could appreciate their desire for such changes, and I engaged in many conversations with them about what this could look like and how best to introduce this style into the church's worship life. I wanted to err on the side of deliberate and careful planning, which, looking back, may have been a little too careful for the taste of some. My concerns were twofold: hold what we did to a certain level of quality and integrity, and approach and communicate what we were doing with the wider congregation with clarity and sensitivity.

As we talked and planned, we seemed to have three options. The first was to develop a second, separate service so that those who preferred one style or the other could choose which to attend. This, of course, has been the most common approach that churches have taken. The second would be to blend modern elements into the existing service, which in my experience can work in the right setting and with intentionality. The third would be to just flip the existing service over to a different style, which a healthy amount of the congregation was sure to reject as soon as it happened.

With the first two options being the most favorable, we came up with a plan. Every time a month had a fifth Sunday, that service would be completely contemporary in style. This would show the congregation what such a service could and would look like if we ever elected to do something on a more regular basis, which in my understanding was the main goal.

We did several things leading up to the first Fifth Sunday Worship. First, we communicated clearly and often what was going to happen, so that everyone would have plenty of notice. Second, we enlisted the help of a local traveling worship band to come in and handle the musical part, which would satisfy my concern about quality. And finally, we left the door open in our communications that this could lead to something more frequent if this service was given enough support by those who'd been wanting this to happen for so long.

The day came, and the service itself could not have gone much better. Members' reactions generally fell into three different categories. The first was the group that made it a point to avoid attending that day: they were not interested in this kind of service and never would be (one member called it "that loud crap," which I appreciated both for its honesty and because it made me laugh). The second group attended out of curiosity: they weren't sure what to expect and what it could mean for the church's future, but they were open to checking it out and talking more about it. The third group was the enthusiastic crowd: they were excited that something like this had finally taken place and they expressed hope that there'd be more to follow.

Sometime during the week after the service, I received an email from one member who'd been part of the push for this worship style. They expressed excitement about how well everything had gone and offered some suggestions for what to do the next time a fifth Sunday rolled around.

Around the middle of the email, however, the tone shifted from one of joy to one of sadness. As happy as they were to see a long-held desire finally begin to take shape, they also recognized for themselves what this signaled. They'd grown up during the pastorate of my predecessor, and, like many around their age, his was the only ministry they'd ever known before my arrival. Not only did my stepping into this role mean a new beginning, but the introduction of a different form of worship—as much as they'd wanted it—was another sign that what came before was passing away.

This member was experiencing a tension between their excitement for the new and their grief for what was passing away. There was a part of their internal selves that wasn't yet ready to embrace a new beginning because they were still working through their feelings of sadness and loss.

As much as people may say they desire change, taking steps to make such changes can bring a mixed and complicated set of emotions. Seeing something different begin to take the place of a former beloved reality will cause people to realize they are carrying lingering grief related to what is passing away. Those emotions may prevent us from accepting such a change for a while, until we can finally come to a place where we have resolved them enough to move forward.

THE NEUTRAL ZONE

When is an ending truly an ending? The answer to this question may seem obvious. Usually, one may say that when an activity stops, an event concludes, one walks out of a job for the last time, or an earthly life experiences death, those are all endings. In other words, we tend to define endings by a tangible moment that happens in time and space. Something happens or exists or lives, and then when it stops happening, existing, or living, that is an ending.

Thus, leaders in the church may make a decision to stop offering a monthly community meal or disband a long-standing fellowship program, and one may naturally think of that as an ending. Likewise, when a minister leaves or some element of worship is retired, those are considered endings.

However, an ending may not seem so clear-cut. And while we could point to a date and time for when an ending happened in a way we could experience through our senses, making peace with that ending may take a while for people who held affection for what ended.

William Bridges and Susan Bridges observe:

> The starting point for dealing with transition is not the outcome *but the ending that you'll have to make to leave the old situation behind.* Situational change hinges on the new thing, but psychological transition depends on letting go of the old reality and the old identity you had before the change took place. Organizations overlook that letting-go process completely, however, and do nothing about the feelings of loss that it generates. And in overlooking those effects, they nearly guarantee that the transition will be mismanaged and that, as a result, the change will go badly. Unmanaged transition makes change unmanageable.[2] (italics theirs)

Bridges and Bridges note that there is more to an ending than just the tangible, spatial moment. There are also psychological, emotional, and spiritual dimensions of an ending that need further attention and intention to bring it to a full resolution.

Due to these additional factors, these authors suggest that a time of transition has three phases rather than just one.

First, there is the ending that we can see and on which we can place a firm date and time. This is the last day when the church serves soup to the surrounding community or the farewell service for a departing minister. During this phase, people acknowledge an ending and begin the process of making sense of their identity when this will no longer be a part of their church or their lives. The time of grieving begins here.

Second, there is what Bridges and Bridges call the "neutral zone." Here the grief may continue, and people begin the process of acclimating to a new practice by virtue of the former practice concluding. In the neutral zone, people start to get used to something or someone no longer being around while learning new routines and patterns that its replacement is establishing.

Finally, the new beginning actually starts. Much like the initial time of ending, the beginning may have already happened in a way that can be measured. The church has already taken on a new mission project that has taken the place of the soup kitchen or the new minister has already begun their tenure, but people needed time in the neutral zone to grieve, to fully accept the ending that has taken place, and to recenter their energy on the new identity and purpose that the new beginning brings.[3]

Ministers find themselves in unintentional interim situations because a congregation is still working its way through the neutral zone after a ministry has ended. If the church had an intentional interim prior to the new minister's arrival, they may have done their best to guide them through the transition period both to help the church resolve its lingering feelings about the ending and to help set up the new minister for a true new beginning, or at least for one to take place as soon as possible.

However, whereas an initial ending may come with a set time that we are able to mark, the neutral zone does not play by such simple rules. It does not come with an expiration date stamped on the carton. Rather, it endures for as long as people need to work through their residual feelings about the ending; to tend to their minds, hearts, and spirits so that they can live into the new beginning that, at least tangibly speaking, has already started.

The hope for an intentional interim time is that the neutral zone lasts for about as long as the person in that role does their work. But it may continue past that point, and the new minister may find themselves facing a need to continue that journey with the congregation for a while. Likewise, for a minister who has helped the church conclude some piece of its ministry and identity that was no longer experiencing vitality, the hope may be that the neutral zone lasts for as long as it takes to start the new activity that is meant to take its place. However, those who took joy in serving or who found it important that the church offer that particular activity may need a while in the neutral zone to make peace with its conclusion.

As with the member who emailed me after our first Fifth Sunday Worship service, many members may even experience a tension between the ending and new beginning. They may be thrilled that the congregation is doing something new, even something they've long believed has been needed for the church to move forward and grow. But they also may be held back by a lingering grief for what has ended; as excited as they are, they may feel a sadness as well.

Many articles may point out all the opportunities that a church can delve into with old paradigms no longer holding up, and both ministers and church members may even agree with them and champion such opportunities to the wider congregation. In the best scenarios, the wider congregation may even receive this vision with the same enthusiasm and express excitement for what is possible. But in the short term, we need to give proper time and attention to working through the neutral zone, or the new beginning may not enjoy deep roots among the people.

SEASONAL SIGNS

When each new season of the year arrives, we have ways of marking its official beginning. The beginning of autumn, for instance, occurs on a day we know to be the autumnal equinox, measured by when the sun will be directly over the equator.[4] This happens during the third week of September, although the particular date varies from year to year. Nevertheless, we can point to our calendars and tell ourselves and others when the first day of fall will be. We use similar methods to name official dates for the other seasons of the year as well.

While many may give credence to this process that combines astronomy with chronological measurement, they may at the same time simply refer to the beginning of September as the start of autumn. September through November tend to be known as "the fall months" in the Northern Hemisphere, regardless of when the equinox comes. It serves as an easier reference point than positioning the tongue to say "September 22 through December 21," even if it may be technically accurate. The third factor may be what meteorological happenings we are used to when we think of certain months. While it is still technically autumn for a majority of December, we tend to associate the entire month with winter due to the cold and snow that we typically begin experiencing with its arrival.

Official times and dates help us make sense of the world. They help us keep deadlines and organize our lives and those of our families. We can name the time on a particular day when we have a meeting, or a day on the calendar when we're set to go on a trip. We use our methods of time measurement not only to mark upcoming events, but to remember past events as well, such as birthdays, anniversaries, and other pieces of our histories most significant to us.

In his book *Four Thousand Weeks*, Oliver Burkeman notes that the way we measure time and seasons today would have seemed strange to past civilizations. Medieval farmers, for instance, would not have had much use for our modern ways of marking time. A typical farmer in those days would have woken up with the sun and turned in for the night at dusk. They would have planted seeds when the conditions were right and likewise harvested their crops months later. It was time to plant seeds when it was time to plant seeds, and it was time to harvest when it was time to harvest. It was time to milk cows when the cows needed milking. Their days were oriented around tasks rather than appointments, and they did those tasks when it seemed best to do so rather than when a clock or calendar told them it was.[5]

Even if we have official dates for when they begin, each season comes on much more gradually, with signs of the new season appearing before the sanctioned marker of its arrival. As mentioned, we may associate either the first of December or the winter solstice with the beginning of winter, but the first snowfall may come as early as Thanksgiving weekend, if not before. While we may say that September 1 or the autumnal equinox is the beginning of fall, we may begin to notice the angle of the sun shifting in mid- or late August, with the earliest changes to the leaves appearing as well. Much like with our medieval farmer, the seasons come and go on their own time and don't abide by our dating system.

This applies to seasons of our lives as well. For certain shifts that we experience, we may be able to point to a date when we made some formal change relating to them. However, like the sun in mid-August or snow in late November, signs of that change came prior to it. A minister may mark their last day of ministry with a church on a particular date on the calendar, but the shifts that helped move the minister to that point began much earlier, and in such subtle ways that they may not have noticed at first. The beginnings of a minister contemplating a vocational change could have happened when a church program didn't go very well or during a particularly difficult conversation with a member, but the minister might not be able to name that until long after the fact. We consider this further in chapter 9.

Likewise, a church can point to a hard date when a program, practice, or ministerial tenure ended. As Bridges and Bridges observe, that may be the official ending, but the ending will continue for a while afterward as individuals and the congregation move through the neutral zone of recognizing, processing, grieving, and accepting this ending. This time of ending is more of a season than a hard and fast day and time. It began before people realized it, and it will continue for a while even after the church has made its formal farewell to it.

As unpredictable as seasons of the year can be, these life seasons can be even more so. At least with the former, we can rely a little more on the cyclical rhythms of the year to anticipate when the next season might begin. Life seasons, however, have less of a rhythm by which we may be able to measure when they may conclude. Causes and catalysts are much more unique and personal to us, going by our own abilities, intentions, emotions, and understandings.

A congregation grieving an ending may be able to do so in the span of a few months. Another congregation grieving that same sort of ending may take longer. And the first congregation grieving a different sort of ending may take longer, while the second may be able to move on from that sort of ending more quickly.

It is not for the minister to decide how long a season of transition will last for a congregation. Like a medieval farmer, they will need to pay attention to the conditions present and till the soil accordingly to help them prepare to cultivate something new.

JOURNALING PRACTICE

1. Inhale a deep breath through the nose, and exhale through the mouth. Repeat this as many times as necessary to center yourself for the practice.
2. Do you recognize the description of the neutral zone that has played out in a past ministry experience? Recall what happened, including your reactions along the way.
3. Are you able to identify a current neutral zone experience that is happening in the life of your ministry setting? What are the factors involved?

4. Describe your own state of mind and spirit as you and your ministry setting are moving through the neutral zone. What do you need during this time? What does it seem others reconciling with their season of grief need?
5. Repeat the breathing exercise until you feel moved to reenter your day. Give thanks to God for this time.

5

Reviewing the Tasks

When the Interim Ministry Network first came into being in the early 1980s, it developed a curriculum to train those who felt a call to this unique and increasingly necessary form of pastoral leadership. The important research done by Loren Mead and others not only inspired a totally new organization dedicated to this work, but specific guidelines and traits that intentional interim ministers should exhibit in their ministry to be effective in this role.

One of the focus points for this new more formalized work was a list of five "developmental tasks" the organizers believe that intentional interims should undertake with churches in transition. They were (1) coming to terms with history, (2) discovering a new identity, (3) negotiating shifts of power and leadership changes, (4) rethinking denominational linkages, and (5) commitment to new leadership and a new future.[1]

These tasks were developed during what I've come to call the "first wave" of intentional interim ministry training. They came about during a time that was still relatively stable for most churches. Many still enjoyed robust membership rolls and solid budgets and attendance numbers. Denominational structures were strong and were churning out resources, statements, and curricula that local churches would choose to use by virtue of being produced "in house," as it were. Cultural shifts in religious devotion had begun but the average congregation had yet to feel them as acutely as they would later.

While some churches certainly would need intentional interim ministers to deal with the fallout of pastorates concluded with an air of uncertainty and conflict, many could still operate with a certain pulpit-warming approach: filling in the gap while a search committee did its work. Chances were higher that an interim could come in to fulfill the usual pastoral needs such as worship leadership and visitation, while also leading some special congregational sessions on the aforementioned five tasks with minimal fuss.

The "second wave" of interim ministry would come sometime in the 1990s or early 2000s. The cultural shifts in religious affiliation would become more pronounced. The "seeker-sensitive" megachurch movement would reach its zenith, and evangelical Christians would solidify as an influential voting bloc. The AIDS crisis would lead to a greater urgency in and acceptance of LGBTQ advocacy. The events and aftermath of 9/11 would heighten a sense of nationalistic fervor and paranoia about nonwhite and non-American populations, as well as a forceful pushback against it in favor of greater inclusivity and understanding of racial and ethnic diversity.

These new developments would lead to increased uncertainty and turmoil in congregations as divisions between members and entire communities became more pronounced. A sizable number of mainline church members drifted to the new mall-sized churches with full bands down the road. Sanctuaries perhaps were still fairly full, though not as full as they once had been. Denominations started having to make difficult decisions about cutting staff and programs. In the midst of all of these shifts, the work of the intentional interim would necessitate a more proactive approach, with the five tasks taking on an increased urgency, yet also with certain limitations arising in how they could be applied.

We're now in the "third wave" of intentional interim ministry, which bears little resemblance to the era in which the "first wave" emerged. The housing crisis and recession of 2008 and 2009 began a time of greater economic uncertainty. The divides that deepened after 9/11 would only worsen in reaction to Barack Obama's presidency and reach an especially low point during and after the 2016 presidential election, which would newly embolden racism, xenophobia, and heterosexism. Both denominations and local churches would continue to experience a decline in resources and commitment.

And then came 2020, when the COVID-19 pandemic would force churches to reimagine how to minister to their members in safe and innovative ways. Divides in opinions between members regarding safety protocols and vaccines would reflect the same differences playing out across the country. In addition, the Black Lives Matter movement would experience a catalytic summer after the murder of George Floyd, with protests happening in communities both large and small. The 2020 election would lead to a new phase of bigotry and violence most clearly exhibited in the Capitol riot on January 6, 2021. All of this would lead to the further erosion of civility in congregations, with members taking out their anxiety on one another, but more so on their ministers. Ministers, meanwhile, would teeter on the edge of burnout while trying to keep churches together in such tumultuous times while also dealing with the worst of member attitudes and behavior.

In this "third wave," the work of intentional interim ministry has never been more critical. The days of merely minding the store in between ministers are long gone. In these current times, the typical congregation is experiencing so much transition and uncertainty that simply keeping the pulpit warm is no longer an option. Not only that, but many settled ministers may be finding themselves in unintentional interim situations: churches with settled ministers may not be experiencing the type of transition that comes between pastors, but there is enough chaos swirling both inside and outside its walls that these pastors nevertheless require the skills of an interim.

The five developmental tasks originally conceived by the Interim Ministry Network have evolved so as to become broader and more flexible to a congregation's situation. In recent years, they have been reconceived as the following: heritage, leadership, mission, connections, and future.[2] These retain some of the spirit of the original five, but with recognition that, just as the needs of a congregation have changed with the wider culture, so must the work of the interim.

In light of the needs of this "third wave," I believe that it's worthwhile to consider each of these tasks. All ministers now find themselves doing some semblance of transitional work whether they consider themselves interim ministers or have gone through the formal training or not. Whether intentional or unintentional, how are these five tasks relevant for today's work

HERITAGE

Interim ministry expert Norman Bendroth defines heritage as encompassing many different aspects of a congregation's history that have contributed to its self-understanding and sense of identity. These aspects include "core values, bedrock beliefs, local history, denominational and theological heritage, and local and world events."[3]

For core values and bedrock beliefs, members might find it easiest to point to a mission statement on the front of the bulletin or hung on the wall someplace prominently. My most recent pastorate, for instance, had a large, polished wood engraving of their most recent vision statement hanging in one of their hallways. As beautiful as the piece was, the statement itself was hardly mentioned during conversations about core values. This may have been due to its sheer length, but also perhaps it was hardly ever referenced after its conception. A mission statement might be a good starting place for such discussion, but if it has never truly taken root in a congregation's life, it may not be the most reliable point of reference.

A better starting place, then, could be to talk about what practices the church has as its highest priority, both past and present. If a church has long had a strong ministry of welcoming and reaching out to first-time visitors, they may be able to name hospitality as a core value. If a church places high priority on offering programs to the community, it may list outreach as a core value. My church had a large activity center that included a gymnasium, and it played host to many sports practices during a typical week, as well as a regular Red Cross blood drive and a Boy Scouts chapter, so we would regularly highlight being a hub for the community as one of our values. Naming these values by observing current actions can be much more informative than reading a statement from times past.

It's important for a church to name important moments in its collective history as part of reflecting on heritage. This could include major changes or updates to the building, moments when the congregation migrated from one building to another, an especially long or notable pastorate, and times of conflict.[4] My church's oldest members still had memories of the previous church building, at which many of them had been married. As I've already noted, when I arrived the church was still processing the end of a long pastorate. These events may have an ongoing effect on the current congregation whether they're aware or not.

Denominational and theological heritage may play a role in the core values and beliefs already mentioned, and it may also inform current decision-making. For instance, churches that became a part of the United Church of Christ when it formed may still refer to their prior identity. This usually will be either Congregational (a more independent-minded form of governance that views wider denominational ties and pastoral leadership as more advisory than authoritative), Evangelical and Reformed, or "E and R" (a more hierarchical form of governance that places greater value in denominational and pastoral authority), or part of the Afro-Christian Convention (a movement of churches rooted in African-American Christian belief and practice that originated in the South[5]). Any of these heritages will have ongoing effects on how the congregation views the wider denomination and its ministry leadership. Churches that formed after the merger and have only ever known themselves to be UCC, by contrast, may have a different sense of these ties altogether.

As noted, some of these heritage elements may be more apparent and obvious than others. Some of them might be clearly stated in pamphlets and on websites. Others might be more dependent on attentiveness to a congregation's behavior.

One of the latest historical events, the effects of which churches are still feeling, is the pandemic. A church considering how it is still shaping their sense of heritage and identity as a result of this event is an ongoing question. They may consider what they did in 2019 and earlier and what has and has not come back as a regular practice. Are they able to offer the same outreach activities as before, and at the same level of energy? If they value hospitality, how are they now doing so in light of health needs and the possibilities that technology brings to expand its reach? If being a community center has long been important, what percentage of the groups from before are still able to use their facilities?

And what has been the congregation's response to this history-shifting moment? Have they approached it as a matter of survival, or of resilience? Have they embraced the new possibilities that this moment has presented, or have they been eager to return to how things were before? Do they view this current time with desperation to preserve something they fear they're losing, or have they resolved to write a new chapter of their heritage for the sake of their future?

LEADERSHIP

Among the changes that churches may experience in times of transition, changes in leadership top the list. This is clearest when a minister departs and the church needs to seek someone new for this role according to whatever process its denomination follows. For churches preparing for a search process, this will include identifying the appropriate gifted person to fill the role during the transitional period.

In this third wave during which there is a higher degree of upheaval and uncertainty and the institutional assumptions that were safe to make a few decades ago are no longer sound, a church will need to spend more time carefully considering the skills of their transitional minister. As even the healthiest churches are faced with more questions of how to do faithful ministry, finding a minister with gifts suited to lead them through answering these questions will be all the more critical. One who is trained as an intentional interim minister should be able to meet these needs for more general transitional situations.

However, a church that is going through a more volatile season that may have particular issues of conflict, dysfunction, or grief may require someone uniquely gifted for the tasks at hand. A church facing a great amount of division may need one who specializes in mediation. A church discerning whether to merge with another or whether to enter the legacy process of closing will need someone able to guide them through the administrative processes that will be involved, as well as to offer care to members grieving what is passing away.

Transitional times may also be times when churches experience changes in lay leadership. Longtime congregational leaders may see the interim time as the opportunity to finally step away from their roles in order to give newer members a chance to step into those positions instead.[6]

As with pastoral leadership, identifying lay leadership includes seeking out those with the gifts, energy, and time for what is needed. Just as a minister called to a transitional position should not just be a warm body to "mind the store," so too should lay leaders be more than seat fillers for the important work of guiding the congregation, especially if it is experiencing a high volume of change.

Part of ensuring that this will be the case entails helping new leaders understand the expectations of their new position through a time of orientation. This could be done during a regular meeting during which time is devoted to reviewing the functions of the group, which can act as a good reminder for longstanding members as well. Or this could be done during a retreat separate from regular meetings, a time for reflection and visioning for the church's future.

In my previous pastorate, the nominating committee approached a newer member about serving on our governing board. He initially agreed and even attended the first meeting for which he was eligible. Shortly after, however, he informed leadership of his decision to step down due to not having understood what the position entailed. I saw this as a communication issue, and I discussed with the board the importance of orientation going forward to help ease newer members into these positions in the future. This served as an important lesson for us.

Of course, congregations and ministers can experience transition without anyone abdicating their positions as well. This third wave of transitional needs carries so much more upheaval that a change in leadership doesn't need to happen for a church to feel its effects.

Right as pandemic-related shutdowns began, I called the president of our governing board to weigh how best to proceed for the safety of our members. Her calmness and concern were evident as we considered our options, and just as many others had, we made the decision to suspend in-person gathering until such guidelines changed. Such calm and concern, along with an anticipation of questions and concerns that would arise after such a decision, would be important for leadership to display.

Congregational consultant Susan Beaumont names a need for congregational leadership to exhibit "Presence," especially during seasons that have a larger amount of transition. Beaumont defines Presence as "a leadership stance born of the authentic self, unencumbered by ego, and led by the Divine."[7] Congregations experiencing anxiety due to a perceived loss of control will need both pastoral and lay leadership who will be able to be honest, vulnerable, humble, and seeking of God's direction. Such a stance will not only provide more stable leadership for churches trying to navigate troubled waters, but it will radiate outward to provide an air of greater stability for the wider membership as well.

MISSION

In his book *Jesus Wants to Save Christians*, author and speaker Rob Bell asks, "If our church was taken away—from our city, our neighborhood, our region—who would protest?"[8] This question is meant to provoke a church to consider whom it serves. Does it exist only to satisfy the needs of its own members, or are there other constituencies beyond its walls for whom it is making a positive difference as well? If your church suddenly disappeared, who would feel the effects of that disappearance, and would they offer lament in response?

This question can be helpful when a church considers its mission. They may reflect on whom they are currently serving both within and outside its walls. They might also reflect on whom they aspire to serve: it may seem strange to consider this, but seeking to widen the circle of those who'd protest a church's disappearance might be effective for certain congregations!

Norman Bendroth states that exploring this focus point involves defining or redefining a church's sense of purpose and direction. It's the positive version of Bell's question: what is a church's reason for existing?[9] Bendroth suggests that a church's mission could be cast in terms of either reviewing or writing statements such as those covered in the preceding "Heritage" section. If a congregation spends time intentionally reflecting upon or crafting these statements, they could be an exercise in answering the questions Bell raises.

Statements about purpose, mission, values, and goals could indeed play a role in clarifying a church's reason for being, as well as how it seeks to serve its own members and its wider community. However, the amount of change and uncertainty in this ongoing third wave transitional season may render the crafting of such statements frivolous. For some congregations, this process may feel like progress without actually meeting the moment.

That is not to say that conversations about congregational identity and purpose shouldn't happen. It just may be that they are now meant to happen in different ways that acknowledge the strangeness of our current times.

Such conversations might reasonably begin with a time of lamenting what used to be, what is passing away, and what is no longer possible. Susan Beaumont calls this part of the process an exercise in attending and surrendering: a time of giving thanks for previous manifestations of a church's identity, even while not knowing what we might be called to next. Even if we haven't yet resolved the uncertainty that this time has brought, we may at least acknowledge that we can't do ministry and mission in the same way while also giving thanks to God for the opportunities to serve in particular ways.[10]

Think of meetings you've been a part of in your church where the conversation has turned to lament for the past: how much fuller the sanctuary used to be, how many more programs it used to offer, how things were when certain members were younger, how a former beloved pastor would minister among the people. This is part of the way a church may work through its season of grief; how it may move through the neutral zone to prepare itself for its next new beginning of service. The trick will be to encourage a church beyond lament so that it doesn't become stuck in its memories.

The work of articulating a church's mission might not be as simple and clear-cut as it once was. It might not come with the writing of statements while sitting around tables. Instead, it might happen in ways that are a bit more off the beaten path from the traditional methods. It may involve noticing what members naturally feel drawn to as they support one another and continue giving their energy to activities that they find enriching. Conversely, it may involve noticing what people no longer feel the need to support with their time and attention.

"A church can't plan a new identity from the safety of the boardroom," Beaumont writes. "We must trust that something important will be given to us that is worth the risk of letting go."[11] The best ways to answer questions about identity and purpose might be more organic. They might involve the invitation to carry such questions around for a while and occasionally report in rather than setting aside a few meetings to hammer out a statement. They will involve ministers sharing what they see happening and helping to steer toward a vision that is already among the people but hasn't been formalized. They may involve individual committees or ministry teams each wondering for themselves who would protest if their church disappeared, and asking how they could do their part to expand the circle.

Mission and identity are as important for churches as they ever have been, but the process of naming them might take new and more creative forms.

CONNECTIONS

The original iteration of this ministry task was to "rethink denominational linkages," but the revisions wisely broadened it to consider other linkages that a church may currently have or has the potential to have. Bendroth defines this task as "all the relationships and networks a faith community builds beyond itself including the denomination, community, and ecumenical and interfaith groups."[12]

As explored under "Heritage," denominational connections are certainly one possible connection. It may be the first such connection that comes to mind, especially if a church has already fostered its relationship to the wider church via participation in regional or national gatherings and projects; regular contact with judicatory leadership, including having them in for church events; and joint activities with other area churches from their denomination. In transitional times such as when a minister departs, a church connected to a denomination will reach out for assistance to search for their successor, as well as for someone to provide leadership in the interim.

While the denomination may have been the primary or even the sole connection to be considered during the first wave of interim ministry, the context, resources, and needs for both local churches and the wider church have shifted so much that seeking connections elsewhere also has become a natural consideration.

For example, as denominational resource centers and publishing houses have elected to make cuts to their educational curricula, local churches have sought out resources elsewhere, including from outside so-called mainline providers. Popular nonmainline series such as *VeggieTales* and Rick Warren's *The Purpose-Driven Life* have been just as ubiquitous in mainline churches as they were in traditions for which they were primarily marketed. Part of the reason for this was the lack of engaging alternatives produced by one's own denomination or by like-minded publishers. As church consultant Richard Hamm observes, "One of the worst-kept secrets in mainline denominations is how many congregational ministers seek the help they need from wherever they can find it, including from sources that might not be 'approved' by denominational executives, when they can't get it through the denomination itself."[13]

These wider connections that churches may seek also extend to physical networks closer to the church's location. As Bendroth notes, this may include local ecumenical associations of which the congregation is a part. While Christian denominational affiliations can still be useful identifying markers for churches, the second and third waves have introduced an increased blurring of lines for the sake of common interests and goals. This may include regular clergy collegial gatherings, the sustenance of a common community mission programs, or projects such as a food pantry or a joint Habitat for Humanity build.

Such connections will also include those beyond churches, including interfaith relationships that function in similar ways to ecumenical ones, partnerships with area businesses, and support to area schools and colleges.

Any of these connections may be long-standing from years or even decades of intentional relationship, and others may be yet untapped. A church in transition may surprise itself when considering just how much potential they have in their area for partnering in ministry.

FUTURE

Bendroth calls this fifth and final focus point the culmination of transitional work. Having explored one's heritage, leadership expectations, sense of mission, and present and possible connections, it is time for a church to look toward the future and prepare for the next phase of its life together. This includes proactive decision-making that will lead to the church taking concrete steps to move toward what it has discerned thus far.[14]

For churches between ministers, this will involve the interim minister and denominational staff each taking responsibility to prepare the congregation for a pastoral search. This will include drawing up relevant documents to present to ministerial candidates, including a list of expected responsibilities and a compensation package, and guiding both the search committee and the wider congregation through that process.[15]

For less conventional times of transition, such as when a minister finds themselves acting as an unintentional interim in uncertain and anxious times, this focus point might be the least clear even if positive progress has been made regarding the other points. Who is to say, after all, when such a transitional time has truly ended—when the neutral zone has been navigated successfully?

Susan Beaumont acknowledges the difficulty of this task. While a congregation may be able to recognize that a former identity is passing away and can even begin to surrender it in anticipation of what will replace it, the inability to see and name that replacement will still bring feelings of grief, anguish, and anger. A minister in this role will be entrusted to guide the church through the fog: "We attend to what is emerging as we walk forward in faith, trusting that a new identity is unfolding."[16]

When so much is left to be discerned, how could a minister and church in transition possibly address this focus point? As with the others, such guidance may simply involve pointing out God's presence and paying attention to where the church is naturally drawn. The results may be more difficult to name and draw up than with a more conventional interim process, and the overall path may have some extra bends in it. And yet, the fact that both sides of the partnership have already discerned that there is a path at all, and thus a future, may be enough to equip each with the hope and faith to keep going.

JOURNALING PRACTICE

1. Inhale a deep breath through the nose, and exhale through the mouth. Repeat this as many times as necessary to center yourself for the practice.
2. Reflect on your experience of the third wave of cultural shifts. How do you see them affecting your ministry setting most acutely? How has your setting responded to any of them? How have they changed your own approach to ministry?
3. Think about the five developmental tasks of the interim. While you may not be an interim in your current ministry setting, which of these may be most relevant or helpful to you and your ministry right now?

4. Take stock of your own internal reactions to our current third-wave reality. What is the state of your own mind and spirit as you seek to minister during this time?
5. Repeat the breathing exercise until you feel moved to reenter your day. Give thanks to God for this time.

6

The Web of the Work

Every church is a system. Or more accurately, it is a series of systems. There is a system of worship: the coordination of greeters and ushers, the planning and scheduling of music, the liturgy and rubrics, the calling of people to help lead.

There is a system of governance: the governing board, committees or teams, how activities both routine and special are planned, how information is shared, how decisions big and small are made.

There is the interpersonal system of the congregation: who has power both stated and unstated, who is getting along and whose relationships are strained, who is connected to whom through blood, business, or friendship.

These and many other systems within a church change over time. Some evolve very slowly, others are subject to instability, still others healthily respond to changing circumstances. All have ways of handling anxiety and tension, some better than others. But there are nevertheless ways of doing things, handed down from one generation of leaders to another. Some are beloved and alive, and they gradually evolve over time, thanks to perceptive participants who wish to see them continue to thrive. Other systems are crusted over by time and inertia, have little energy, and fade away when the last few dedicated organizers finally give up.

One thing that changes most often in church systems is the staff. This includes clergy, ministry coordinators such as those for Christian education or youth, administrative professionals, and custodians. Some of these positions change more frequently than others. But congregations call and entrust certain work and leadership to individuals who have credentials and skills and who are compensated accordingly.

As mentioned in an earlier chapter, new staff people enter the ongoing stories of the congregation, and thus they also enter a series of established systems. Naturally, both staff and system are expected to get along; indeed, that expectation contributed to the former being called or hired to begin with.

Of course, the actuality of this expectation tends to be more complicated. Both staff and system are used to certain practices; both believe in a best way of accomplishing tasks and making decisions. Along the way, there is bound to be some give and take, some measure of compromise as they all move ahead in ministry together. Usually, it is the staff who are expected to learn the system before suggesting changes, which the system in turn may first attempt to process (and suppress) via whatever learned mechanisms it has in place to manage anxiety. If there is enough diplomacy on the staff's part and enough willingness to experiment on the congregation's part, this can be overcome.

Sometimes, one or the other will go into business for itself. A staff person will discern that it will be more efficient and worth spending some social capital to handle something on their own. At other times, the system will change or be changed without the staff's input, and staff, regardless, will be expected to function successfully within the new arrangement.

Like any successful partnership, the keys to the system and staff working well together are trust and communication.

The system has been around for a while. It's not perfect by any means, and sometimes it's downright dysfunctional. But there are real people involved—at times caught up in it—with desires and dreams and uncertainties and hang-ups. And while they aren't perfect either, they're doing what they know how to do and have the best interests of the church in their hearts and minds.

The staff also know a thing or two. They have training, experience, and knowledge; they've been around. They certainly aren't perfect, either; they have just as many quirks as the people who have called them. And they, too, are doing what they know how to do and have the best interests of the church in their hearts and minds.

So if all of these imperfect people with their preferences, habits, and hopes are meant to work together, then they need to trust that the other knows something about what they're doing and discern when it's best to just let things play out. But that also entails communication, one to the other, about what needs to happen or what is going to happen. It entails talking to one another about what may be best for the church's future, when one or the other is planning to move forward in some fashion, whether the change that one makes will really be workable for the other, and when it really will be best to go through the hard work of forging a new path together. This "third way" will involve a change in the system and the staff's preferred methods.

But if the two expect to be together for a while and want the other to succeed, then the third way will be worth it.

NO LONGER ALONE

Near the end of my time at my first pastorate, I encountered a pastoral situation that I thought I had the resources and wherewithal to deal with on my own. A combination of my own stubbornness, naiveté, and selfish hope that things would resolve themselves quickly led me to take this route, and I'm still processing those mistakes all these years after they happened. I'll save the specifics for another book. For our present purposes, I'll simply say that (1) this situation included factors too wide and deep for any person in ministry to handle on their own, no matter their gifts and expertise and (2) I tried anyway.

I arrived at my second pastorate still wounded by what had happened. I was still trying to work through my decision-making and their results alongside acclimating myself to a new ministry setting. I was walking into a system still grieving its former minister and unpacking what a future without him would look like, but I was also bringing the emotional and spiritual aftermath of my former pastorate with me. Coupled with my family's experiences with churches during my formative years, I was far from a neutral party as the specific pastoral needs of this new congregation presented themselves. I was bringing my own background, experiences, biases, skills, shortcomings, and wounds to this new place of ministry.

I was at least partially aware of the baggage that I was lugging behind me as this new chapter began. For instance, I wanted very much to avoid my family's past experiences that came with following a longer pastorate, and so I took deliberate steps to address the issue when it arose and to treat its unspoken effects even when no presenting issue was happening. I had also learned my lesson about trying to tackle mountainous pastoral situations by myself, and so I resolved to entrust others to share the burden when necessary. And it did become necessary on a frequent basis.

One of the first ways I shared the burden was to talk to the former pastor directly. This wasn't just done by my initiative: he reached out to me more than once as well, hoping for a path forward due to his own love for the church he had served for so long. We met once at my house, and a second time with our Association Minister at a coffeehouse to assess the best way to help the church through its current moment. This included establishing an understanding that pastoral needs should be referred to me as the one officially now called to the position, and discussing best practices to handle times when that would occur. Our Association Minister also suggested a formal recognition of this ministry transition via a liturgy during Sunday worship, which we took to be a worthwhile thought but never enacted.

These conversations made a positive difference in several ways. First, it invited leadership from the wider denomination in as an active and aware partner in the work. While they would not be an ever-present participant, it did help to have them as someone with more distance from the situation able to provide observations and consultation. It also provided the former pastor with a better understanding of his role moving into that of friend and referent. Going forward, I received more than a handful of calls from him letting me know of issues he'd been approached about first, and in the majority of these cases the party that contacted him was able to shift their former dependence on him to me.

The church's Spiritual Council[1] also became a conversation partner in the work, as the congregation's needs regarding its ongoing relationship with the former pastor became an occasional topic, either by their initiative or my own. In several cases, I'd pass along discovered instances of when members approached him about pastoral concerns, which would serve as opportunities to clarify the council's work in helping the congregation continue to move into a new understanding of relationship both with him and with whomever was currently and officially serving in the pastoral role.

Perhaps the biggest opportunity to do so came a few years into my tenure, when one council member shared that they'd been asked when the former pastor could be invited back as an active member. The understanding by the one asking would be that he'd be seen as a fellow member and friend rather than in his former role. This wasn't the first time I'd heard the question myself, and, given my family's history and what had transpired during my time at the church thus far, I had my reservations.

However, I saw this as another opportunity both to discuss the issue with leadership and keep this a team effort, and to help members continue to work through their grief in this neutral zone season. So I asked what effect the council foresaw this having on the church, as well as reiterating my own concerns given what had already taken place. The conversation was productive and further clarified our work together as spiritual caregivers.

Given these conversations, I made several conclusions. The first was that indications pointed to a downward trajectory in requests for the former pastor to step back into his former role. The second was that certain forces and factors were present such that a refusal might cause more damage in both the short and long term. And finally, I was willing to trust both my leadership and the membership at large that this could be done in a healthy way.

Leading up to Christmas Eve that year, I handwrote an invitation to the former pastor's family inviting them to worship that evening. They accepted and have continued as active members since. There did continue to be times when all parties involved needed to navigate the complexities of member feelings regarding his presence and role, but given the imperfect and dynamic nature of ministry, this is how we proceeded.

For my own part, I took solace in not only knowing but accepting and living into the fact that I wouldn't have to deal with such complexities by myself. It was a lesson borne through painful trials and errors and one I'd have to continue to figure out case by case. This would be our "third way," for better or worse.

THE MANY PARTS OF THE WEB

As I've already discussed, each church is a series of systems. It is first its own system, which includes how it makes decisions, whom it has empowered or disempowered through both official and implied means, and how it maintains order. As I discussed in chapter 4, this system also includes the congregation's ongoing story—its actual history, the story it reiterates among its members, and the story it wishes to present to newcomers and outsiders. These are often three distinct stories to more removed observers.

Newly called ministers step into all three of these stories and their accompanying systems. Initially, they will be one of those removed observers and are likely to react accordingly. They may be able to appreciate the ways a church touting itself as "welcoming" is living up to that self-designation but will also see behaviors that work against it. They may celebrate along with a church that loves to highlight its community outreach and advocacy but will also see ways to improve. They may hold reverence for a church that prioritizes its ties to history and tradition but will also be able to name its need to remain relevant to the issues of the present.

The COVID-19 pandemic provided a unique and powerful disruption to these systems and stories, both highlighting and accelerating ways in which they each were not meeting the needs of both members and communities. Even so long after most churches have returned to many practices and activities they knew and loved beforehand, questions about participation and viability are ongoing.

This is an opportunity for self-reflection and discernment that ministers shepherding them through such times will inevitably find challenging, exhausting, and possibly isolating. As with all helping professions, the work of ministry has always had the potential to exact an emotional toll from its practitioners. This toll can be made even steeper if a minister attempts to address a difficult set of circumstances by themselves.

As I've shared in my own story, an attempt earlier in my ministry to act as a heroic Lone Ranger figure taught me some hard yet valuable lessons that I carried into my next pastorate. The very first indication that I was encountering another such challenge caused me to put these lessons into action by reaching out to numerous people and groups both within and outside the church for guidance and support.

I've come to call this vast combination of systems, stories, and support "the web of the work," based on my best understanding of how a spiderweb functions. If you touch one strand of the web, you'll inevitably affect other parts through the vibration that it will cause. No part of the web exists separately from the rest; all of it is connected no matter how far apart. True, the parts that are closest will feel an effect most immediately and experience a more significant impact, but the parts more removed will still be affected, if in no other way than to hold fast while another part needs greater attention due to distress or damage.

Both minister and congregation—-as individual members and as a collective body—occupy their own spaces on this web that includes many more than just themselves. They are each affected by the movement that these other entities cause, just as their own actions impact the others. Likewise, a minister or church may also seek reinforcement or support in times when their spaces feel weak or threatened.

A minister facing the unique and increasingly difficult pastoral needs of the present moment will be aided not only by considering the web of the work in which they are a part, but also by reaching out to other parts of the web to help avoid isolation, loneliness, and burnout.

The preaching scholar Thomas Long notes that when one ascends the pulpit to preach, there are many more parts to the sermon than whatever notes or manuscript the preacher brings with them. And these various parts each are dynamic, changing week to week and moment to moment. As a result, the sermon is a living, breathing event rather than mere words written and spoken, where each of these parts swirl around one another, reacting and changing and recoiling and receiving what happens. Long writes:

> Preaching does not occur in thin air but always happens on a specific occasion and with particular people in a given cultural setting. These circumstances necessarily affect both the content and style of preaching, but if we think of preaching as announcing some rarified Biblical message untouched by the situation at hand, we risk preaching in ways that simply cannot be heard.[2]

The preacher must have a working awareness of these moving parts both when preparing what to say on Sunday morning, as well as while actually saying it.

Such a sentiment may also be applied beyond the preaching event to the entirety of the ministry partnership. The web in which both minister and congregation find themselves is also moving, reacting, changing, affecting, and being affected by the other factors within and beyond.

Long names four parts of the preaching event: the congregation, the preacher, the sermon itself, and the presence of Christ.[3] When taking into account the parts of the ministry web, we can name quite a few more:

The Congregation. I've talked quite a bit already about the systems and stories already active in any congregation and into which the minister will step, as into a moving stream that began further into the woods and continues down to an unknown destination.

To complicate this part of the web even more, the congregation not only includes its collective system and story, but the many systems and stories that members bring with them from other places. This includes family of origin, the system of one's current family whether biological or chosen (or both), identity, successes, struggles, uncertainties, questions, and so much more. And each of these individual dynamic parts are also reacting to and trying to make sense of their experiences inside the church as well as in the wider world to which the church is called to minister. It truly contains multitudes.

The Minister. As much as the minister may try to remain neutral, unaffected, and undifferentiated from the congregational system and from individuals who present needs, there is only so much they may be able to do in this regard. The minister inevitably brings their own history and context to the pastoral moment.

This may include memories of past similar situations that continue to live on in their mind and body. Depending on how well those instances had been resolved, the minister may feel a pull to apply those circumstances and enduring emotions to this new time and place in ways that may be unhelpful or inappropriate. These have the potential to cast a presenting situation with preconceived notions that are not warranted or give a minister a felt need to overcompensate with a response that is more rigid or distant than necessary.

This may also include concerns about life events, past or present, outside of one's ministry responsibilities that are nevertheless affecting their thoughts and feelings. This may include worries about family or finances or unresolved trauma from a childhood experience, among other possibilities.

This part of the web will also include the way that the minister's body and mind live in the world. People of different races, ethnicities, economic backgrounds, sexualities, gender identities, physical abilities, and mental health challenges will have different reactions to the world around them, as well as experience different responses and biases from others. This especially will be the case if the space in which they are ministering is not predominantly similar in background. If the "default" of a ministry setting is that of a white, straight, gender binary worldview, a minister who does not match that in one or more ways will bring different knowledge, wisdom, and experience.

All of these parts of who the minister is can bring an opportunity for growth, learning, and blessing for the congregation, but usually not without effort that they will need to undertake for themselves. In the meantime, the minister will need healthy supports after a pastoral encounter, especially if they have had to put in the extra work of addressing unchecked prejudices.

Denominational Polity. Any church-related support and guidance that a minister may receive will depend on the structure and governance model of both the congregation and the denomination (if any) to which the church belongs. Denominations that are more hierarchal in structure may be able to apply processes more easily or offer policies during times when the minister or church needs them. By contrast, a structure that gives greater power and autonomy to the local church may have less to offer by way of accountability or assistance. A particular system will also have different ecclesiastical and theological freedom and restriction for decision-making that may either be preventative or provide greater organization for when it is needed.

These sets of policies and structures will have an inevitable influence on the relationship between the minister and the church. An awareness of the wider church's stances and resources may affect choices made in the moment, as well as how each party may proceed afterward, especially if one or both determine that mediation will be necessary. How that mediation takes place and how direct the wider church is able to be will differ and may be more or less helpful in a given situation depending on specifics.

As mentioned in an earlier chapter, the resources provided by my denomination, the United Church of Christ, strongly recommend practices that limit a former minister's contact with a congregation. However, for various reasons, that may not always be the path chosen by the parties involved. Our congregational structure gives enough leeway for this path to be an option, and so this option will require additional guidance and attention in other ways.

Wider Church Staff. Related to denominational polity is the availability of regional or national denominational staff for intervention, advocacy, guidance, and support. Once again, a more hierarchical structure may be able to wield greater influence in times of conflict, whereas more congregational structures may hold the church to more indirect ways of involvement.

Whatever the circumstances of governance, however, denominational staff are still entrusted with the work of providing resources and best practices for ministers and congregations seeking to improve their partnership. Even in structures that give greater deference to local churches, there are often still processes through which healthy dynamics are encouraged or reaffirmed.

In my particular situation that I shared earlier, I had several options even in a tradition more congregational in nature. First, regional staff was willing to meet with the former minister and me to discuss the best path forward in our unique circumstances. Second, our regional Committee on Ministry would be available with a process at the ready for situational support if it was necessary.

Regardless, keeping wider church staff updated with each new turn in this ongoing issue would at least keep them apprised of what was happening between both a church and a minister for whom they were entrusted to provide care. It would also be another avenue through which a minister could transfer at least some of the burden of this pastoral situation off their own shoulders.

The Minister's Internal and External Support Structure. In the best of circumstances, it is only to the minister's benefit to work alongside relevant individuals and groups within the congregation to address the church's needs. This includes approaching the appropriate committee, team, or volunteer group about beginning a new ministry initiative or making changes to an existing one rather than trying to tackle the issue by oneself. It also includes bringing larger issues related to the church's systems or stories to leadership and working with them to discern the best way to address them in healthy and life-giving ways. This could include the church's new identity that is emerging as a result of pandemic-related changes, or how to continue guiding a congregation through the neutral zone of grieving a former minister's departure even while a new minister has begun serving among them.

Beyond the need for reaching out to others to partner in the shared work of ministry, a minister also has the need to find support for their own mental and spiritual well-being. A minister who intentionally tends to their own health has a much better chance of engaging in healthy ministry.

Some of this support does have the potential to come from within the congregation, although a minister must be very aware of appropriate boundaries. The dynamic of the minister-congregation relationship should not be such that the minister should feel free to vent to one church member about another or share extensively about some hardship in their personal life with the expectation that a member should provide support as a counselor or friend would. These sorts of instances risk exploiting the pastoral relationship in harmful ways.

The primary way in which a congregation may be able to provide support will be through a Pastoral Relations Committee or equivalent group by another name. The Ministerial Excellence, Support, and Authorization Team of the United Church of Christ offers this definition:

> The purpose of a Pastoral Relations Committee, or PRC (sometimes called PPRC, for Pastor-Parish Relations Committee) is to support the healthy relationship between pastor and congregants in order to promote healthy, faithful, shared ministry. It does this in two primary ways: by serving as an advisory group to the minister, sharing ideas, dreams, expectations, and concerns of the congregation with the pastor; and by serving as a support group for the pastor's leadership, interpreting roles, functions, boundaries, opportunities, and needs of the pastor to the congregation. PRCs are places to help the minister and the congregation maintain appropriate expectations for the scope of the minister's work, and for the pastor to be able to test visions and receive support for their continued growth in ministry.[4]

A Pastoral Relations Committee is a group that offers advocacy and support to the pastor and helps them maintain a healthy relationship with the congregation. A Pastoral Relations Committee that honors its role will help improve the pastor/congregation relationship, increase morale for the pastor by assuring them that people have their back, and enjoy a better performance of ministry tasks as a result of said morale, among other possibilities. This group has a unique and necessary calling in the congregation. This is meant to be the primary form in which a congregation may provide internal support for its minister.

Beyond the congregation, a minister has many more options that may tend to their needs in a variety of ways. First, there is the minister's family and friends. They may not be able to know or understand every detail of the minister's experience with their ministry setting, but they will be a source of love and supportive relationship. They are under no aforementioned restrictions regarding venting, and they will be among the most knowledgeable regarding the minister's personality, needs for comfort and reassurance, preferred ways to blow off steam, and favorite snacks.

A minister may also turn to professional and collegial support. One option already mentioned is denominational staff, who will be able to provide some guidance in a more official capacity. Another is any formal or informal network of fellow clergy who know the struggles that can come with ministry and can provide companionship through listening, advising, and prayer.

Finally, a minister also has options beyond the work of ministry to receive sustenance for emotional and spiritual needs. This may include regular meetings with someone in the mental health field—a psychologist or therapist—who can provide dialogical and medicinal help. This may also include a spiritual director who can encourage the keeping of a regular prayer life and the continual cultivation of a relationship with God.

The web of the work is extensive. An awareness of its numerous parts can help us gain a greater awareness of all the active factors present in ministry. It will also give us a better understanding of and appreciation for the resources and support available to us as we seek to serve in the most faithful and healthy ways possible.

JOURNALING PRACTICE

1. Inhale a deep breath through the nose, and exhale through the mouth. Repeat this as many times as necessary to center yourself for the practice.
2. Write your name on the center of a page. Then write down all individuals and groups whom you consider to be part of your own Web of the Work on the paper around your name. Encourage yourself to use the entirety of the paper for this and resist any urge to neatly organize them such as listing them to one side. Draw arrows between your name and each of theirs.
3. Reflect on the relationships that each of these parts of your web have to one another. Draw arrows between those whom you believe have their own connection.
4. Consider the arrows between your name and each of theirs. How have they provided encouragement, support, and resources to you, or how might you need them to regarding a current ministry situation? Consider the arrows that connect them to each other: how might those connections be of benefit to your ministry in your current season?
5. Repeat the breathing exercise until you feel moved to reenter your day. Give thanks to God for this time.

The Congregation's Story

It didn't take me very long after I started serving in full-time ministry to realize that something about the way we do church needed to change. There was no single incident that caused this realization for me. There was plenty to affirm that I'd faithfully followed my calling, and I enjoyed both the tasks of ministry and the people whom I'd been called to serve. But I also picked up a sense that the church was losing its central position in societal organization, something that had been transpiring for decades by that point.

I noted this in member commitment: church activities at one point may have commanded greater attention on the family schedule in the past, but work, school, children's activities, and other personal and social enjoyments now largely took precedence over Bible study or youth group.

I also noted this shift in terms of how younger generations in particular would participate, when they actually had the time and interest. Whereas those of a certain age could be counted on to attend, help with, and support church activities in droves, those in Generation X and younger did not share their parents' and grandparents' enthusiasm for making the church their primary social hub. They had other groups and methods of interacting around common interests, and they preferred them.

Having observed all of this, I concluded that the church—the particular one I was serving, but also American mainline denominations in general—needed first to recognize its waning privilege and influence, and then to consider how to meet the emerging new reality in which it was finding itself.

I had plenty of resources and perspectives at my disposal as I considered the nature of that need, both its cause and potential solutions. From social media to church-related blogs, books, and articles, ministers and other church workers are regularly subject to analysis and pontification about *what the church should do.*

What the church should do to attract/retain young people. What the church should do to serve the poor. What the church should do to be relevant or authentic or whatever the current buzzword is that basically means "attractive to cool people." What the church should do to engage their communities. What the church should do to engage and welcome minority voices. What the church should do to truly be postmodern.

All of these resources purporting to break down the factors involved and proposing better ways to do and be church were refreshing, and they reassured me that, yes, the church has a future as long as we pay attention to the data and to successful case studies where these sorts of principles were applied.

There came a point—and, really, it was inevitable—when I'd become so steeped in these sorts of resources that I began to feel a little worn down. Part of that is just sheer volume: every time I turn around there is a new study, a new voice, a new perspective, even as the content begins to sound very similar. But there are a few other elements at play for me personally.

The first thing is simply that I've tried some of it and failed. Books and articles proposing *the new better way to do church* don't include "failure stories." They don't include the story of the new church start that folded after eighteen months. They don't include the story of the pub discussion group that fizzled out. They don't include the attempts at "radical hospitality" that ended up becoming an unhealthy, uncomfortable mess of unregulated boundaries.

There are several reasons why these books and articles only share the successes. The most obvious one is that failure doesn't sell, so these stories need to be weeded out or ignored. The second is that a lot of this pontification hasn't actually been tested in any real way. Of course the church should be out serving local communities in mission, engaging younger generations, welcoming the outcast. These important goals are easy to talk about in sermons, classes, workshops, writings, and conferences. The trouble comes when you move from saying to doing. And the third reason is that the writer may have been able to catch lightning in a bottle due to contextual factors lining up perfectly for them, but their model is difficult or even impossible to replicate anywhere else.

Those within the church—especially those entrusted with any kind of leadership or consultant role, including myself—often lament how awful it is that the church is not yet the ideal "Kingdom Come" on earth, and ask why haven't we yet achieved the unregulated perfect lovefest that it's meant to be? There's an easy answer for it, easier than many think, and it begins with another question: Have you actually tried to do it?

Human beings are experts at getting in their own way. We have hundreds of years of prejudice and oppression to untangle. We have the mental and emotional needs of many to account for. We each have our own unchecked biases, unrealized privilege, and unresolved issues to acknowledge. It's amazing that anyone could have a high theology of the church given that it is made up of people.

Having spent a lifetime in the church, there finally comes a point where all of the armchair quarterbacking that begins with the words "The church should just . . ." rings more and more hollow for me, because attempting it quickly reveals that there is no such thing as "just."

So then, what about the churches that have actually achieved a worldly measurement of success? This is a fair question. Do touted models such as small group ministry or coffeehouse worship or Organic Church have a path to success in every setting in which they are attempted? The likely answer is no, because not every setting is ideal for every single one of these ideas. Size, location, congregational energy, and a hundred other factors need to be read well to discern what might really be appropriate.

And really, that's what it comes down to: local context. "Contextual" was a buzzword for a while, and it is one of the more enduring and appropriate ones. Every local ministry setting has its own flavor, its own needs, its own grouping of personalities and hang-ups. And these unique factors in each place end up rendering "the church just needs to. . ." sorts of statements relatively useless. General principles may be helpful, but once on the ground the realization will come that it is going to take more paying attention to a local situation and less to every latest "visionary" book, every daydreaming church guru on social media, every new study, to figure out what is meaningful and what is going to work there.

These issues have taken on an even more complicated character since churches had to scramble to see to their members' needs in early 2020. Ministry settings faced new questions about how to keep people safe, how to increase use of technology, and how to hold the community together. In the years since, churches have had to continue to evaluate their continued use of technology, how to reach back out to members who haven't returned, and how in general to be in community with one another given that the ways people gather and relate to the church have taken on new configurations. And some who remember what their church was like prior to the pandemic may be angry, anxious, or sad that it hasn't yet returned to that state of being.

Many of those former ministry theories and methods don't seem so robust anymore, because the world to which we are called to minister has changed. What does church growth look like now, or does that question even matter in the same way anymore? Do the old arguments about traditional versus contemporary worship still need to be hashed out in the same ways? What does church membership look like or even mean now?

It's helpful to hear what others are doing, or at least what others have tried. It's helpful to engage voices from other places. But there comes a point where we need to move from saying to doing, from reading to serving. And in the midst of the failure and the weird mix of people we have to work with and the disillusionment and basic trial and error, we operate with the hope that maybe some piece of God's realm may really appear, if only for moments at a time.

Most churches are still navigating a season newly informed by lessons learned during the pandemic and where importing models seems much less important, because the context of each has changed so much. Many may still share through networks what is working best for them, and that has been a beginning. But there may be a lot of failure along the way as ministers and churches continue to try to figure this out, and that's okay.

REFRAMING FAILURE

The story I am telling in this book did not turn out the way ministry books typically present the application of their models and ideas. My realization of the work before me in my new pastoral role did not lead to a clean, linear series of easy decisions and victories around helping the congregation move forward in embracing new pastoral leadership. It wasn't that simple, and unlike the polished versions told in many books of this kind, they never truly are.

The phone call that I received my very first day requesting that the former pastor return to conduct a loved one's funeral was the first of a handful or more such requests that I would need to address in the first few years there. This was actually helpful to me in the sense that it disillusioned me of the thought that no such work would be required of me, and so I was able to be more attentive and prepared for when these incidents arose.

Given that my predecessor's style and approach to ministry was all that the church had known for a quarter century, comparisons between his and my own preferences were inevitable, from worship leadership to my approach to educational programs to visitation, and even to how I organized my office. Some of these comparisons would be made to express a preference, while others would be to show surprise at the difference. Still others would just be to inform me what people were used to in instances when I wasn't familiar with a tradition.

I relied so much on trial and error when navigating this unintentional interim work. Not only did I feel ill-equipped to handle this transitional chapter, but I was also trying to do it while carrying my own family's history of encountering similar instances in the past that led to short pastoral stays, hurt feelings, and residual suspicion. I was very mindful of emotions caused by childhood experiences and wanted to avoid repeating what caused them. I was also aware that this task fell to me whether I wanted it or not, for the sake of every individual who would serve in this pastoral position after me.

Perhaps my biggest failure in those earliest years was not recognizing just how much the cultural shifts around church involvement were gaining speed. For some, the end of the previous pastorate was their cue to take their spiritual commitments elsewhere. Others would drift away or join the ranks of the nones or dones over time. The beginning of my ministry there saw attendance numbers in the range of 120–140, but attrition due to these changing factors would see those numbers decline over my tenure.

It was difficult not to take this as a personal failing, even given the larger circumstances of church commitment across the board. I frequently would ask myself whether anything I myself was doing could reverse these losses or engage new people to make up the difference. I had plenty of books full of suggestions and success stories, but none of them seemed to fit our needs. The ones I did use—adapted for context—seemed to add meaning to our congregational life, but none were the magic solution that they often promised to be.

A feeling of failure can contribute to an attitude of scarcity and risk avoidance. If one thing doesn't live up to expectations, we may on the one hand accept the instance of disillusionment and recalibrate for the next time. But on the other hand, we may not know how to respond and instead become fearful of trying again. In addition, we may internalize those failures as indictments of our own abilities, which can affect other areas of ministry for which we've already displayed competence or giftedness.

Times of failure often need to be reframed, so that we may more accurately assess it, respond to it, and move forward from it. Such a reframing may happen in a number of different ways.

First, when a minister is called to a church, they are joining a story that began long before they arrived. This story began at the congregation's founding, and has been shifting, changing, and evolving ever since. Every birth and death, every member added and lost, every cultural movement that impacted it, and every choice made both monumental and seemingly miniscule has shaped this church's story over years, decades, and even centuries. That history has shaped the current dynamics of the church's life whether it realizes it or not and continues to influence its self-image. These influences are at work when a new ministry initiative is proposed and implemented and will impact how it takes shape, whether with enthusiasm for it or resistance to it or apathy against it. As much as the minister may wish otherwise, they are only able to control a small portion of these influences, if any of them at all. If a church activity or event brings results that don't meet expectations, the dynamics of this continuing story may not have yielded the right set of factors for it to produce fruit.

Another way to reframe failure is to consider where this congregational story may yet go sometime in the future. A minister may dream of introducing different elements of worship, establishing a new outreach to the community, or taking a stand for an important justice issue, but they may not be able to make much headway with membership to see it happen. However, it may be that sometime after the minister's tenure concludes, another leader encounters a slightly more receptive dynamic—including the seeds planted by their predecessor—that may allow for greater movement toward that dream after all. What a minister may immediately see as a failure may have helped till the soil for something life-giving in a later season.

As mentioned in the chapter on disillusionment, failure can be reframed in terms of losing an illusion of what the church may be capable of or open to doing. That loss of an illusion will lead to greater clarity regarding what may be possible in the present moment of this church's life. The minister also may be able to reframe this moment of disillusionment as an opportunity for learning a little more about the ministry partnership, and to regroup and grow as necessary for it to continue.

Along with this loss of illusion will come a need for the minister to show themselves gentleness and forgiveness. When they see something they believed in falter or not catch people's imaginations, it often comes with a lot of frustration, anger, sadness, and disappointment. And this can also cause the minister to blame themselves and doubt their calling and gifts. Once again, recall that any particular minister is only a small part of a church's story, one that stretches much further both into the past and future. While important to acknowledge and process the negative emotions that moments like this will bring, it is also important to realize how much more is at work beyond your own control.

Enough of these sorts of events over time will nevertheless cause a minister to engage in some reflection regarding both their call to their present setting and their call to ministry at all. They may initiate a time of discernment to see where else they may be called to serve, or they may sense a depletion of interest, energy, and inspiration for their work, which are signs of burnout. These possibilities will be discussed at length in chapter 9.

MINISTRY IN NINEVEH

In his book *Under the Unpredictable Plant*, Eugene Peterson interprets the story of Jonah in light of the pastoral vocation. Jonah is told to prophesy in Nineveh, a detestable city in many respects (another prophetic book in the Hebrew Bible, Nahum, refers to it as a "city of bloodshed"). Jonah shares in this hatred of Nineveh, to the point where he resists God's call to go there. In fact, he doesn't just pretend that he doesn't hear God or put off going. Instead, he heads in the opposite direction, boarding a boat to sail to another place called Tarshish.

Peterson describes Tarshish as an exotic place full of culture, romance, intrigue, and adventure. It certainly was preferable to Nineveh. So that's where Jonah decides to go. Of course, he never makes it. A storm hits, he has to be thrown overboard, he prays in the belly of a big fish, and eventually he does go to Nineveh where he belongs.

Pastors, Peterson says, all want to go to Tarshish. Tarshish is a paradise, with wonderfully perfect and obedient congregations serving in all sorts of efficient, polished ministries. But, he continues, "Tarshish is a lie."[1] Spend enough time in one church, and you will quickly find that it's just another Nineveh, filled with imperfect people struggling with their own lives (to say nothing of their church commitment). So a minister may face the temptation to buy another ticket and look for Tarshish somewhere else.

This approach to congregational ministry lacks an appreciation for place, for context. Peterson observes that a pastor can't engage in ministry without the specifics of where they are located. Ministry is about these people in this place right now, rather than some ideal group of people somewhere that ultimately doesn't exist. He even goes so far to encourage a reverence for place and for the particulars of people's lives—to help identify where God is even in the midst of the mundane, the mediocre, and the tedious.[2]

When times of disillusionment or failure happen, this temptation to seek out Tarshish may grow even stronger. A minister may struggle with feelings of inadequacy in themselves, but alongside those may come wonderings about whether they'd be better off in a different ministry setting. If an idea for serving in ministry didn't work out in one context, perhaps it will in another.

A minister may reach a point where nothing further can be done, when the time truly comes for both sides in the partnership to part ways. Peterson does acknowledge that, but states that pastors should weigh whether that is really the case, or whether it's just a valley in a series of peaks and valleys.

Ministry, especially in these pandemic-informed times, involves a lot of walking with a congregation in their anxiety, despair, or joy, and not only showing up but actually helping them make a connection between their ongoing story and God's story. To do that, a minister may need to be willing to stay put for a while, to appreciate and love where one is in all its particulars, brokenness, and imperfection. Tarshish is a lie; Nineveh is where God wants us.

In the middle of my seventh-grade year, my family moved to the place that I've continued to call my hometown. For the previous five years or so, we'd lived in the parsonage next to a rural church in the same county; I'd basically come up through elementary school during that time. I'd already experienced two moves (three really, but I have no recollection of the first one) by that point. Five years is a lifetime for a person at that age. I'd basically planted roots for myself, had made some good friendships, had come to love the freedom of the wide open spaces in which our house was located. It really did seem like I'd lived there forever, and my secret hope was that I could.

Unfortunately, it was not to be. This was the church at which I'd answered the phone and heard an anonymous voice state that my father's ministry wasn't appreciated. Remaining in that parsonage wasn't an option due to how things had degenerated between the church and my family. Staying in the area wasn't an option due to financial restrictions and other factors. So we moved to another new city, another new house, another new school system, and another new life.

The memory of the night my parents broke the news of where we'd be moving continues to be vivid in my mind. It was an accidental thing; I think they'd meant to approach a moment like that with more care and finesse. Instead, my father was on the phone with somebody discussing the move, which had apparently been settled. I overheard this, turned to my mom and asked where we were going. After being told, I ran to my room screaming

"No!" I knew full well that this would mean starting over yet again, and I didn't want to. I was tired of starting over. Five years in one place had been forever for me, and I hadn't wanted forever to end.

It did end. We moved, and I eventually settled in at our new place. I found friends; I found my first serious girlfriend. By the time I finished high school, I'd lived in this new place for five and a half years. Strangely enough, this time it didn't seem like forever. I saw an ending coming. By my junior year I was starting to look at colleges. I knew that further change was going to happen and was preparing myself for it. I did so again during my senior year of college. I did so again my last year of seminary.

Change is inevitable. It was a painful lesson for my seventh-grade self, but that lesson came more easily as I got older. It seems like my entire time serving in pastoral ministry, I tried to learn the opposite lesson. My first pastorate lasted eight years, and up to that point it was the longest that I'd lived anywhere in my entire life. My second pastorate lasted seven years, and even after departing that ministry we've continued to live in the same city, the same house, and the same school district, and continued the same life. There's no designated ending for this: no graduation, no culmination, no decision to move looming from somebody else.

Ministers who remain in the same ministry context for more than a few years begin to anticipate those feelings of sameness: eventually will come another movement through the familiar themes of Advent and Christmas, of Lent and Easter; of vacation Bible school, and of other annual projects and programs. Over time, ministers get to know the rhythm and routine of their contexts by heart. They know what to anticipate and when to start planning for upcoming seasons.

In the long story of a congregation's life, seven or eight years is not forever. On a minister's "low days," it may seem like forever. But in a vocation where the average stay for a pastor is four years,[3] seven or eight years—let alone ten or twenty-five—can seem like forever.

In ministry situations that show signs of being unintentional interims, even a few years may seem too long, let alone the average or above average amount. If a ministry's primary tasks include helping a congregation through unresolved conflict, trauma, or grief, even a year or two may feel like much longer. And if it seems to feature a great amount of what outwardly looks like failure, it may seem long enough.

However, a process of discernment may reveal that this is still the Nineveh to which we are called for a while longer. This will bring natural questions as to how to continue sustaining oneself for the duration of one's time there. I will remain true to my earlier observations regarding books that propose foolproof magic solutions complete with success stories of those who have implemented them. When it comes to what a minister needs to sustain themselves, it turns out that there aren't any never-before-heard methods. Instead, the basics still work best.

In his book *In It for the Long Haul*, Glenn Ludwig reflects on what a minister needs to sustain a longer pastorate. He proposes five pillars on which to build a foundation for doing so, which I'll briefly recap:

1. ***Monitoring burnout***—Continually finding meaning in what one does and managing stress. Strategies to deal with burnout include maintaining spiritual practices, taking time off, seeking support networks, getting exercise, and so on. Again, burnout will be addressed in chapter 9.

2. ***Balancing individual and corporate needs***—Building trust with individuals and also instilling confidence in the congregation as a whole; not letting the small group of chronic complainers run your ministry; recognizing when a program has reached its endpoint even if an individual wishes it would remain.

3. ***Balancing power and decision-making***—Inviting new people into leadership; keeping congregational democracy alive by welcoming a variety of opinions and people; sharing leadership and delegating responsibility.

4. ***Seeking quality feedback***—The longer a minister is at the same church, the more clergy evaluations may be about laypeople not wanting to hurt the pastor's feelings or not being able to see their growing edges. Ludwig suggests more of a shared evaluation process of each ministry as opposed to a one-way evaluation of the pastor's performance.

5. *Sustaining growth, seeking depth*—Essentially, keeping the three poles of ministry, family, and one's own spiritual formation in balance; recognizing that studying a text for a sermon is not personal Bible study, writing a prayer for worship is not personal prayer time, etc.[4]

None of this may sound new or ground-breaking. It may be that your theological education or your denomination routinely tout the importance of self-care and boundaries, or that you're already a regular part of a collegial group of some kind. If you have one or more of these practices in place, certain times may call for you to lean more heavily upon them, including right now.

Whether one's ministry is currently thriving or struggling, experiencing outward success or failure, or exhibiting the marks of a healthy settled pastorate or an unintentional interim, the fundamentals provide the foundation. The small daily acts of self-care are still the most important, just as small daily acts of ministry may compound over time to make proper space for larger visions to come to fruition. These small things will also increase the chances of playing a longer part in the congregation's story.

JOURNALING PRACTICE

1. Inhale a deep breath through the nose, and exhale through the mouth. Repeat this as many times as necessary to center yourself for the practice.
2. What is a recent or current ministry situation that has brought about a feeling of failure? Reflect on what happened, including your own internal reactions as it played out.
3. Consider the ways to reframe failure suggested in this chapter: (1) the dynamics of the larger congregational story that are out of your control and (2) the unknown future for which the current moment may have been a seed. In light of these factors, what need do you have for gentleness and forgiveness, and how can you show that to yourself?
4. Reflect on Glenn Ludwig's five pillars. Which of these seem strongest in your ministry right now? Which of them might require additional support from your Web of the Work?
5. Repeat the breathing exercise until you feel moved to reenter your day. Give thanks to God for this time.

Practices for the Journey

When I began ministry in my second pastorate, I had brought several practices with me that I found to be sustaining for my body, mind, and spirit. They were invaluable to my health and growth as a person and had taken on additional significance as I sought balance between my call to ministry and the other areas of my life.

The most consistent was a regular writing practice. I began journaling the summer before seminary. It proved to be nourishing during those formative years, as well as later when I was called to my first pastoral position and as my family grew. Shortly after my first settled call began, I also started a blog, at which I first wrote almost daily before settling into a less frequent though still regular routine.

With both pen and paper and keyboard and pixels, I used this creative outlet to chronicle my daily experiences and reactions to life events, reflect on ministry experiences, keep notes from books and conferences, and record ideas for other creative writing possibilities. Sometimes this time of writing would include explicit articulation regarding God's presence in the midst of these happenings, but at other times the whereabouts of the divine would be left to implication or for interpretation after more time had passed.

This practice survived many major life transitions and endured from one pastorate to the next as well.

The prayerful dimension of this practice was one of several contributing factors that would inspire me to enroll in a program to be trained as a spiritual director. The seeds were planted during my seminary years, and I had mulled this possibility for years until I finally found a program close enough to me. During my initial interview to be accepted into the program, the director recommended that I hold off a year from formal classwork. During this delay, I would be guided through the *Spiritual Exercises* of Ignatius of Loyola—the backbone of this particular program—both for my own edification and to get a better idea of what I would eventually guide others through.

This recommendation turned out to be quite providential. I found the *Exercises* to be an enriching journey through the life of Jesus. It would introduce deeper ways to approach and experience scripture and deepen my understanding of meditative prayer. It also would turn out to play a pivotal role in my discernment of a call to a new church, even if the actual transition would take a little longer to happen.

My spiritual direction studies would accompany me to my new call, and I made sure to bring up this commitment early in the process so as to make proper space for them to continue while orienting myself to a new congregation. The search committee affirmed my involvement, voicing the importance of continuing education for any individual who would be their pastor.

The second year of my program included a practicum, during which I would need to meet with directees of my own finding for a certain number of hours. I decided that an easy way to fulfill this requirement would be to offer an abbreviated form of the *Exercises* to interested members of my new congregation. In addition to satisfying the conditions of the program, it would also give me a unique opportunity to get to know the congregation. And sure enough, members younger and older, working and retired, took advantage of this offering.

After I was formally certified as a spiritual director, I continued to occasionally offer these individual sets of meetings. My newfound learnings also would affect my ministry in other ways: how I wrote sermons and led worship, how I offered educational opportunities, and how I approached pastoral care situations. It would also have a lasting deepened effect on my personal spiritual life, including how I journaled and wrote, as well as my approach to prayer.

Spiritual direction would also have several effects on my interests in professional ministry. My meetings with congregants were one expression of a longstanding desire to help churches explore the possibilities of spiritual practice beyond Sunday worship, to help Christians become more aware of the breadth and depth of spirituality in our faith tradition far beyond the single sliver with which most are familiar. As mentioned, I tried to do this as often as I could.

This longstanding desire would also play a role in my first opportunity to publish a book. It would be yet another expression of my wish for mainline denominations in particular to explore spirituality beyond what most are used to: to expand their horizons beyond the "three hymns and a sermon" model that many congregations in these traditions know best.[1]

One other regular practice that I found (and continue to find) sustaining was physical exercise, which I began during my seminary years and continued to pursue after beginning full-time ministry. For the most part, this would consist of walking around the cemetery adjacent to my first church, or jogs around it when the weather was warm. My family eventually invested in an elliptical machine, which we brought with us when we moved closer to my new church. After that machine was no longer usable, I made greater use of our YMCA membership to use their ellipticals or treadmills.

The biggest shift in my workout practice would come when my wife and son signed up at an area martial arts dojo. They originally did so as a bonding activity for the two of them, as well as a way for our son to learn confidence and discipline. In those earliest months, they would begin encouraging my daughter and me to try it out ourselves, which I initially resisted because I wasn't sure I'd be willing or able to make the time. Eventually, however, I caved.

The earliest lesson I learned after stepping onto the mat was the need to unlearn the politeness and hesitation that we internalize as we become adults. I was encouraged to yell, to move my body in ways I hadn't since my school days, and, yes, to actually hit and kick other people (with the proper amount of control).

Other lessons would follow that would expand my appreciation for my own physical self. It would help me realize that my body could do more than I'd thought possible. It would also teach me how to move or refrain from moving, to exercise greater discipline over my body, which would also involve greater discipline of my mind. These lessons would also permeate my practice of ministry.

I could not imagine what my years of pastoring a church would have been like if these spiritual, physical, mental, and creative practices had not been a part of my journey. For me they were life-enriching, artistically satisfying, beneficial to my overall health, and essential to my personal growth.

Those who are involved in any form of ministry need such practices for their own wellness for this work.

NO, REALLY, TAKE CARE OF YOURSELF

I've just described a few of the practices that I have found meaningful and impactful for my own well-being. One or more of them may resonate with you, or conversely, you may not be able to imagine yourself taking one or more of them on as your own. I share them merely to show what has worked for my own journey toward a sense of wholeness and renewal, rather than as a prescription for others.

Ministry always carries the potential to wear down those who serve. Years ago I heard someone describe the toll that ministry can take being primarily mental or emotional. This makes sense, as people in ministry often walk alongside others in some of the most difficult, heart-breaking, and anxious moments of their lives. Not only that, but we may also help to mediate contentious meetings, navigate opposition to new initiatives, spend our own energy trying to stir up that of others, and address the minutiae of administration and office concerns.

This may wear down our minds and emotions first, but that in turn will also affect our spirits. We may become so bogged down by the concerns of the church that we lose track of God's presence with it all, which may lead to an increased disconnect with our sense of call. Such fatigue and tension will also live in our bodies, putting increased stress on our muscles, joints, nerves, and organs.

Ministers who have been in this work for any length of time have heard many a reminder to take care of themselves. This tends to include encouragement to be firm about your time away, find stimulating activities outside of ministry, balance work concerns with those of family, keep a regular prayer practice, and any number of other specific practices that are meant to maintain your health. We've perhaps heard these reminders so often, in fact, that they begin to lose impact. We already know the importance of self-care in theory, but we nevertheless may face problems putting it into practice.

The rest of this chapter will lift up the importance of ministers caring for their health in four areas: the mental, the physical, the spiritual, and the creative. There are many other people and media that prescribe specific practices to address each, and everyone will have to undertake their own trial-and-error experiences to figure out what works best for them. My goal in highlighting each of these areas is merely to show how a constant mindfulness of each may help motivate us to put theory into action in the pursuit of a healthier life.

THE MENTAL

To attend to one's mental health is to ask, "What's happening inside?" This includes paying attention to one's immediate internal reaction to an external event. It includes how one processes and reflects upon that event—including those immediate reactions—later on. It includes delving into what deeper factors may be contributing to those reactions and processing. And it includes practices that address what parts of any of those things might be unhealthy while upholding healthier options for the future.

First, the immediate internal reaction. If some element of a situation causes us discomfort, we may respond in a way that acts on our interest of self-preservation. These are often categorized in popular discourse as "fight," "flight," or "freeze." If our reaction is to fight, then we become adversarial, argumentative, and act out of a felt need to launch a counterattack either verbally or physically. In this case one may tend to blame the other for our reaction, and we may even voice that blame as part of our defensive action.[2]

If our reaction is flight, we will do our best to shrink away from the perceived threat. This response will cause us to downplay what is happening, or to appease or placate the other person. The flight response desires peace at all costs, even if the other person's behavior is problematic. Flight will cede ground to problems rather than address them.[3]

Finally, if our reaction is to freeze, it may look similar in some ways to flight, but also involves more of a retreat into ourselves. We may dissociate from what is happening around us, our body or mind shutting down to avoid further interaction or reception of the external threat.[4]

What causes us to react in one of these ways in any given difficult situation? What was happening inside us during that interaction? We may not be able to name those factors in the immediate moment, but we may have a better opportunity to do so later after it has passed, when we are aided by the distance of time and perspective. At this point we may be able to name ways in which we were reminded of something in our past that was similar and the effects of which still cause us pain. We may be able to name learned behaviors from long ago that we have not yet been able to address.

This in turn might help us name what deeper habits, memories, or trauma we still carry with us that contribute to unhealthy reactions or coping strategies. Both this piece and the later processing of the event may best be done with someone who is trained to walk that road with others, such as a counselor or therapist. And if it is determined during these sessions that one might be aided by medication to bring one's thinking back into balance, the counselor will be able to provide referrals for that important component as well.

Such processing and taking of prescriptions may be two helpful practices for the betterment of your mental health, but others that may be helpful in the immediate moment include breathing or prayer exercises. Others include regular practices that help you release built-up energy, such as a form of exercise or martial arts, or practices that help you wind down, including warm baths or massages.

Such practices always should be evaluated in terms of how much they contribute to your well-being. If a practice carries the danger of making your health worse in some way—routine excessive alcohol consumption, or a therapist who seems to dismiss your concerns, for instance—then you will need to exchange it for something else.

The key to greater mental health is both to analyze what is going on inside of you, and then to find regular, healthy methods of tending to it.

THE PHYSICAL

While on my sabbatical, I visited a retreat center. I had a loose idea of what I would do while I was there and brought some materials in a backpack with intent to read and journal, among other activities. But for the most part, I felt content to just let the time happen and enjoy being in a place set aside for reflection and rest.

After a while, I visited the chapel, which had a simple modern aesthetic including an altar, podium, and cushioned wood chairs lined in rows. I sat in a chair to allow myself time to settle into the space. I observed my surroundings, I listened, I took deep breaths. Eventually, I closed my eyes.

And then I had a strong urge to lie down on the floor.

I can best describe this urge in terms of how imagining lying on the floor caused me to feel. It seemed like it would be so relaxing, much more so than sitting would be. If I could just sink down onto my back, a message in my mind kept saying, that just would be the best thing I could do.

So I did. I lay down between the rows, and my view became nothing but the wood ceiling and a single overhead light. And, sure enough, my physical urge turned out to be the correct one. It felt natural to be in that position, much more so than if I'd forced myself to remain in the chair. I'd needed to take a position of rest, and my body sent me strong signals to get me to pay attention.

In her book *Finding Your Own North Star*, Martha Beck talks extensively about how our bodies send us clues about what we really want and need to be healthy and whole:

> The unconscious portion of the human mind communicates through symbolism when it creates dreams, language, and every form of art. It can also express itself symbolically by acting its messages out with the body. Not always, but often, a physical problem is a coded message from the essential self, a dramatization of needs or problems the conscious mind can't or won't articulate.
>
> New Age gurus claim that certain injuries always have the same meaning for every sufferer: Psoriasis means something's "gotten under your skin," leg injuries are always about lack of social support, an achy-breaky elbow indicates that you don't have enough freedom,

> and so on. I prefer the diagnostic criteria Jung used to analyze dreams: I think every person's brain creates its own symbols. . . The owner of the body is the only person who can accurately translate its symbolic symptoms.[5]

Beck also observes that we have received so many messages to (1) ignore our feelings in favor of our rational abilities and (2) do what would get us the greatest positive social feedback. So when we have any inklings to the contrary, we tend to downplay them as much as possible. This includes physical reactions or impulses.[6]

Think of when you've been in uncomfortable situations and you start to feel unease in your stomach. Or times when you enter the building to go to your job you don't like and you feel a tightness in your shoulders. Or a particular person you don't get along with starts talking to you and your muscles tense up.

Perhaps our first reaction is to not listen to our body. Again, we've been socialized to not react in ways that would embarrass us, or to keep powering through hard times at work, or to be polite no matter how repulsive we find someone to be. We might reassure ourselves that it's just nerves or we're just tired, or to power through for the sake of satisfying internalized messages about not upsetting others (ironically, these are also all physical messages that we'd be using as excuses to downplay other physical messages).

These are all times when our body is telling us something; pointing us in a different direction, telling us that the path we're on or the situation as it currently stands is not healthy for us. Sometimes it's as simple as an impulse to lie down on the floor.

If there had been other people in the chapel that day, I might not have listened to what my body wanted. I would have remained in my seat to seem socially proper and not risk upsetting anyone else in the room. But I would have been ignoring what I really needed.

Our bodies know when something in our lives isn't working, or is dangerous, or is wearing us down. They know before our minds and felt social obligations will allow us to understand or act. They will let us know when something needs to change, whether it's our immediate surroundings or some larger part of our lives that is keeping us from living into our true core identity.

When we need certain things, our bodies will tell us. What difference would it make if we let ourselves listen? What new path could we discover?

THE SPIRITUAL

Early in Ignatius' *Spiritual Exercises*, he introduces what he calls the First Principle and Foundation, a lengthy statement about humanity's purpose on which the *Exercises* are based. It is a mission statement of sorts by which practitioners are meant to live to pursue joy and fulfillment rooted in an awareness of God. A contemporary translation of the First Principle and Foundation begins like this: "God who loves us creates us and wants to share life with us forever. Our love response takes shape in our praise and honor and service of the God of our life."[7]

People in ministry may use similar language when making vows to serve at special times that authorize their ministry, such as ordinations, installations, or commissioning services. Ministers have been called into a unique form of service and are reminded of that whenever a new chapter in their vocation begins. God has placed a particular calling upon ministers, and our love response, as the First Principle and Foundation states, is to return thanks through acts of praise and service.

Of course, Ignatius did not mean for his *Exercises* to apply only to clergy or people in religious orders. His statement is a general application for all of humanity, because God's loving presence includes all whom God has created. And so even if one hasn't discerned a call to authorized ministry of some kind, that same love response is meant for everyone.

For those in ministry, the need to nurture one's spirituality is just as critical as it is for anyone else. We may have the tendency and temptation to believe that since we are already immersed in regular worship, Bible study, and prayer by nature of our work, we are already keeping a robust spiritual life. We may think that we're already giving our love response every day just by showing up to work, and there isn't much more that we need to be doing. It is easy to just be going through the motions, to have the routine down pat, without any kind of spiritual stirring or passion happening in our heart and soul.

Jesuit writer William Barry makes some additional observations about the First Principle and Foundation. He writes, "We do not know and love and serve an abstraction. To ground a life and a relationship, these statements must be the distillation of experience."[8] Words about our love response to God are meant to have an experiential component to them so that we move beyond the abstract to something that is more real to us. Spiritual practices beyond the work of ministry can help us cultivate a vibrant and inspiring awareness of God.

There is no shortage of such practices from which to choose, and many books, articles, retreats, and conferences exist that can explain them all in incredible detail. I've already mentioned how much the practice of journaling has meant to me over the years. Others may find that something different works for them. One may even find that a practice not traditionally known to be "spiritual" may nevertheless be what helps them gain knowledge and experience of God's presence in their life.

Thomas Merton also believed that such practices could extend beyond the most traditional forms:

> Learn how to meditate on paper. Drawing and writing are forms of meditation. Learn how to contemplate works of art. Learn how to pray in the streets or in the country. Know how to meditate not only when you have a book in your hand but when you are waiting for a bus or riding in a train. Above all, enter into the Church's liturgy and make the liturgical cycle part of your life—let its rhythm work its way into your body and soul.[9]

Whatever practice we may choose, the more important thing is nurturing that awareness of God's presence. And not only that, but a practice is not only meant to be for the time that we have set aside for it during a given week, but its effects are meant to last beyond that time, seeping into the rest of our day such that even the most mundane activity can be viewed through the lens of God's creative love playing an active part. This will keep our ministry life from stagnating, but it also will ensure a healthier spiritual life in general.

THE CREATIVE

The movie writer and director Guillermo del Toro wrote a book titled *Cabinet of Curiosities*, which is a collection of entries from his notebooks where he works out ideas for his films, as well as explanations for how or whether they were used or changed or filed away for later.

In addition to sharing artwork and writing he'd composed while working on these projects, del Toro also shares a little about his approach to moviemaking, as well as his general philosophy about creativity. At one point, he is quoted as saying:

> "One of the biggest lessons Leonardo [da Vinci] leaves for all creators is that man is the work of art," notes Guillermo. "Obviously, the Mona Lisa is a masterpiece. The Vitruvian Man, The Last Supper—both masterpieces. We can all agree on that. But Leonardo—the man, the anatomist, the designer, the architect, the scientist—is the real masterpiece. He is his ultimate creation. So live well. Be curious and hungry and always in awe of the world."[10]

The nature of ministry is that of an art rather than a science. It involves adaptation to changing circumstances and new challenges. By virtue of the nature of how humanity shifts and grows and reacts and moves, ministry necessitates a generous amount of creativity to respond to its needs.

To be effective in ministry is to be creative. Creativity involves, as del Toro observes, a curiosity, hunger, and awe of the world around us. This engagement will not only help us to see the ever dynamic beauty and tragedy of life, it will also nurture the creativity needed to respond to it. Each will feed the other.

There's always a danger in ministry, and in life in general, to become comfortable, bored, and disengaged, to reach an inner space where we never feel challenged to grow or to try new ideas. This is one of the dangers of disillusionment, for instance, when something we thought was possible doesn't go how we hoped. Enough loss of illusion may cause us to give up on any continued pursuit of trying new things.

Years ago, I was talking to a friend who at the time was going through premarital counseling in a group setting, and there was a pastor in the room who kept interrupting the presentation to give long-rehearsed bits of wisdom about aspects of marriage. To my friend, this pastor seemed less engaged in the material and more content to say the same things he'd perhaps been saying for twenty to thirty years.

What seemed to strike my friend most about this was how it seemed like this pastor wasn't even trying any more. He'd found his comfortable spot in this area of ministry, and was going through the motions, perhaps out of obligation or fatigue. But it certainly wasn't out of a place of creative stimulation or engagement.

Ministerial entropy is a danger all pastors face. It's part of the reason we're encouraged to take continuing education time and pursue hobbies: the former continually develops ministry skills or introduces new ideas long after we leave seminary, and the latter keeps us stimulated by things other than church work. These are really two sides to the same coin: stimulation inside and outside the church is important for pastors to keep growing professionally and personally.

One way to push back against entropy is to engage in creative pursuits outside of ministry. I've already named a handful of practices that help me do this: journaling, writing, and martial arts. You may be able to name your own, whether you're currently doing them or whether you've always had an untapped interest. This could include playing an instrument, yoga, knitting, cooking, woodworking, cars, and theatre, among so many more that we could name. These activities engage our creativity, which in turn helps us look at the world in increasingly creative ways.

Author and creator Austin Kleon writes, "The first step toward transforming your life into art is to start paying more attention to it."[11] If it is part of the minister's job to help others see where God is at work in members' lives, it takes creative visioning to do so. Creative activities outside the church will help nurture that within us.

JOURNALING PRACTICE

1. Inhale a deep breath through the nose, and exhale through the mouth. Repeat this as many times as necessary to center yourself for the practice.
2. Write four lines across a page. Label one "Mental," one "Physical," one "Spiritual," and one "Creative." Using a scale of 1 to 10, where 1 is the least satisfactory and 10 is the most, how would you rate each of these parts of your life. Be honest with yourself.
3. List practices that you currently observe for each of these areas. In addition, create a "wish list" of practices that you don't currently observe

but would like to. What's one thing that you can do in the next week to pursue one of those items?

4. Reflect on how current practices (or lack thereof) are affecting your ability to do healthy and effective ministry in your current setting.
5. Repeat the breathing exercise until you feel moved to reenter your day. Give thanks to God for this time.

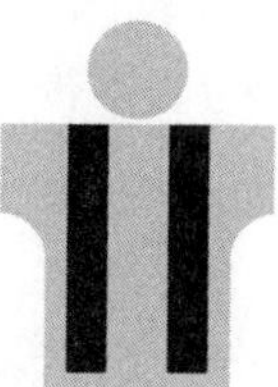

[illegible] would like to [illegible]. What's one thing that you can do in the next week to pursue one of those tasks?

4. Reflect on how [illegible] attentive [illegible] enhancing your ability to do [illegible] and effective ministry [illegible] setting.

5. Repeat the breathing exercise until you feel prepared to re-enter your day. Give thanks to God for this time.

The Call Cycle

The story of Abram (later Abraham) in the book of Genesis is one to which many turn when seeking stories about unwavering faith in God. Abram's call story at the beginning of Genesis 12 is brief, and yet holds great power for many due to its lack of hesitation or questions.

> Now the Lord said to Abram, "Go from your country and your kindred and your father's house to the land that I will show you. I will make of you a great nation, and I will bless you, and make your name great, so that you will be a blessing. I will bless those who bless you, and the one who curses you I will curse; and in you all the families of the earth shall be blessed." (Gen. 12:1–3, NRSV)

In a few verses, we first have God summoning Abram to leave behind everything he knows and loves. He is called to give up safety, security, and standing and go to an unnamed land that God plans to give to him and his offspring, which will be so numerous as to become an entire nation. As a result of the creation of this great nation, Abram's own name will also become great, forever remembered due to what God will do for the entire world through this new established people.

A crucial promise is embedded within these other promises: God will provide Abram and his wife Sarai (later Sarah) with a son. They have been unable to conceive over the course of their relationship and now they are advanced in age, well past the years when such a development would have been possible. Yet the birth of an heir is necessary for these grand divine promises to come to pass. As incredible as the prospect of a great nation and great name to result from Abram's response is, his and Sarai's ability to have a child is even more unbelievable.

And yet, Abram does as God commands. He picks up his entire life and follows God into an unknown future. He hasn't even been told where he's going, and yet he goes anyway.

Again, this story is lifted up as a model of faith for future generations to emulate. From the Apostle Paul and the writer of Hebrews onward, many a preacher and teacher has pointed out the amount of trust that goes into such a move, exhorting hearers to be just as trusting of God in all things.

But Abram's journey turns out not to be so straightforward. On several occasions, Abram's faith does waver, and at times that wavering brings harm, sorrow, and trauma not only to himself but to his household. In several attempts to avoid negative repercussions from the rulers of the lands in which he temporarily settles, he pretends that Sarai is his sister. In one attempt to produce his own heir apart from what God has promised, he has a child through Sarai's slave Hagar, and both she and her son Ishmael almost perish in the desert due to Sarai's jealousy. Abram's story of faith is more complex than that initial story of call and obedience in Genesis 12.

One of Abram's earliest moments of wavering faith occurs at the beginning of Genesis 15. He has already been through some hardship on his new journey, and the trust he exhibited in that first instance of response is fading. No signs of a promised heir, let alone of a great nation or great name, have yet manifested, and he's beginning to wonder if he made the wrong decision. God sees this and comes to Abram to provide reassurance.

> After these things the word of the Lord came to Abram in a vision, "Do not be afraid, Abram, I am your shield; your reward shall be very great."

> But Abram said, "O Lord God, what will you give me, for I continue childless, and the heir of my house is Eliezer of Damascus?" And Abram said, "You have given me no offspring, and so a slave born in my house is to be my heir." But the word of the Lord came to him, "This man shall not be your heir; no one but your very own issue shall be your heir." He brought him outside and said, "Look toward heaven and count the stars, if you are able to count them." Then he said to him, "So shall your descendants be." And he believed the Lord; and the Lord reckoned it to him as righteousness. (Gen. 15:1–6, NRSV)

Abram's call story has more components to it than that first moment of acceptance. In these six verses, we see several others play out.

First, Abram experiences doubt. Nothing he thought he was responding to has happened yet. Sarai has not become pregnant, and thus no biological heir has appeared. Instead, he is facing the prospect of his inheritance going to another member of his household whom he will have to adopt.[1]

While we can't read too much into Abram's thoughts in this passage, such doubt may have led to other thoughts, such as whether to go back to what he left behind. If that was not an option for him due to custom or circumstance, he may have considered settling somewhere of his own choosing for he and his wife to live out their remaining years. The consideration of abandoning this call for a path he'd forge himself had to have been at least enticing for him.

Next, Abram openly questions the status of his calling. He brings his concerns and questions to God with honesty. Whether he receives an answer or not, he feels comfortable enough to name how he's feeling to the one who brought him out here to begin with. He has followed God's lead due to a promise, so where's the promise?

Next comes God's answer to Abram's question in the form of a metaphor. God leads Abram out to look at the night sky, unsullied as it would be today by the lights of parking lots and streets and buildings. God challenges Abram to count the stars that he sees above him, which are so numerous as to make counting them impossible. This is how vast Abram's descendants will be, and it will happen through a natural heir rather than an adopted one. If God can create such a far-reaching universe, God can also do something as far-reaching as provide Abram a son.[2]

Finally, Abram's call is reaffirmed. This interaction is enough for Abram to continue trusting in God's leading and promise. Abram's faith is renewed that his feeling of barrenness will eventually be overcome by God's fulfillment.[3]

If Genesis 12 is Abram's call story, we could consider Genesis 15 Abram's discernment story. Long after that celebrated moment of acceptance, trust, and following, Abram has come to a point where he needs to discern whether his current path is still the right one. Included in this time of discernment is doubt, questioning, honesty with God, reading the signs around (or in his case, above) him, and reaffirmation.

All of these elements show up in various ways when people of faith engage in their own process of discernment. Sometimes one eventually feels called back to what they're already doing. Other times, they discern that it's time to do something new. And if a great model of faith like Abram, whose calling seemed so guaranteed, occasionally went through such a time of discernment, the rest of us are certainly bound to do so as well.

THE CALL CYCLE

A sense of calling does not remain in a single state for the entirety of its existence. Rather, it is a living thing, dynamic and shifting. The person who senses a call will change, going through times of growth and joy and hardship and self-reflection. Likewise, the setting to which one feels called will change as circumstances, resources, energy, and people involved change. And, as both called and place of call go through these shifts, the interactions and responses between the two will as well.

As a minister experiences these shifts, they will go through times when their sense of call will be clear and times when they will question whether that call is still viable and life-giving either for themselves, their setting, or both. This will take on a cyclical nature in which a minister will experience peaks and valleys in energy and in their sense of connection to God's Spirit.

Here is each step of the call cycle:

Affirmation/engagement: A minister feels excited about what they are doing and where they are doing it. The sense that one is called to serve among this particular group of people for such a time as this is strong. Furthermore, the minister feels a closeness and gratitude to God for the work, gifts, and presence that they are able to use and experience in their present setting. As a result, the minister is highly engaged and also feels gratitude for where and how they are currently serving.

Creativity/productivity: A natural byproduct of high affirmation and engagement, the minister in partnership with their ministry setting is able to generate a lot of ideas and energy for both existing and new ministries. They are able to see ways to improve what is already being offered, as well as begin developing new initiatives for both the congregation and the surrounding community.

Stability: The minister and their setting come to a point where they are more focused on maintaining what they worked on during the creative/productive stage. Energy levels off as the focus becomes keeping the ministries they believe in going as best they can.

Decline: Now the energy is starting to trend downward. Ministries don't even have the plateaued energy that they needed to keep running smoothly. Maybe volunteers who were helping to run them have decided to step aside and nobody has been eager to take their place. People, including the minister, are beginning to feel tired, worn down, or bored. The minister may even feel a shift in that closeness and gratitude that was so prominent in the affirmation/engagement phase, wondering why they don't feel the same way now.

Evaluation/discernment: Finally, the minister comes to a point where they realize they need to step back and reflect on what they and the ministry setting are doing together. They look at ministries that seem to be faltering, and they examine their own physical, mental, emotional, and spiritual energy levels. This is a stage where the minister engages in discernment about the future of their ministry, and whether it should continue among these same people or if they should begin a new ministry elsewhere.

Opting out or going back to affirmation/engagement: This is the crossroads point, depending on the outcome of the minister's discernment. They may decide that they are called elsewhere and the ministry setting would benefit from new leadership and opt out, eventually beginning a new cycle with a new set of people. On the other hand, they may discern that they are to continue in their present setting and, in the process, feel a reaffirmation of their ministry among them. The latter will bring a renewal of the gratitude and connection that they'd lost track of during the decline stage, and they will become newly engaged in the work of ministry. And the cycle begins anew in the same place.

When we reach the less energetic and affirming stages of the call cycle, there are ways to engage in them that will help once we reach the crossroads of discernment and evaluation.

First, we may ask what potential the ministerial relationship may still have. This may include an evaluation not just of one's own sense of call to a ministry setting, but also of what is happening within that setting. Have certain programs and ministries reached the end of their viability, or can they be reimagined? Does it seem as if there may still be new paths to forge together if the relationship can find its creative footing again? Does the minister have need of renewal or healing; could that happen while continuing to serve in the same place, or would leaving be one of the initial steps that brings it? Asking about remaining potential is a central piece of discernment.

Second, in the more positive stages of the call cycle, one may engage in internal shrine-building. When an affirming moment happens in ministry, make special note of it. These moments may be celebrations, such as an ordination or installation service, or particularly life-giving moments, including a successful church event or an especially meaningful pastoral care moment. We may not only remember these moments but may build shrines to them in our spirits so that when less affirming, critical, or harmful moments happen, we may return to them and remember that, despite the negativity of the current time, we still have a calling and God is still with us as we pursue it.

Third, the stage of discernment and evaluation may include testing the possibilities of being called elsewhere. For traditions that use a search process for ministers, this may include dipping one's toes into the search waters. Just putting your call into written words in a ministerial profile or spoken words during an interview can provide further clarity as to whether you are called to something new or back to where you already are.

Finally, discernment isn't meant to happen in isolation. Rather, a minister should rely on the web of the work—colleagues, spiritual directors, family, mentors, and the like—to listen and help name what the minister is experiencing during this phase. They will be able to point things out that the minister cannot see, affirm the minister's gifts, and lovingly push back if the minister seems to be avoiding certain factors. Discernment is for the individual, but it is also meant to be communal.[4]

Viewing a sense of call as a cycle can help us recognize where we are in the process, the characteristics of the stage we're in, and ways to tend to our internal and external needs.

MY OWN DECLINE AND DISCERNMENT

When it became clear that our Fifth Sunday Worship experiment was set to come to an end, a variety of internal and external factors began to weigh on me with increasing force.

By the time this ministry offering ended, a number of members had moved on or stepped away from active participation in the church's life. There wasn't a single cause for this ministry's ending as far as I could tell, but I could identify several primary reasons. First, those continuing to feel grief over the loss of the previous longtime pastorate decided it would be best to close this chapter of their church involvement and seek fellowship elsewhere. For some this happened before or shortly after my time with them began. For others it was a slower process that was finally completed several years in.

For others, the Fifth Sunday idea wasn't leading to more. Our area has an abundance of larger churches with established modern worship services, and those options became increasingly desirable as opposed to continuing on with the uncertain and experimental status of what we were doing. This group included many younger families and most of the people who had wanted something like Fifth Sunday to begin with.

Still others began to count themselves among the "dones." I heard more than one person say that they needed a break, or that there were other things happening in their lives that were beginning to need more of their attention.

And still others were beginning to stay away due to my own ministry mistakes. While I hope that they were not above a rare or average amount, I did occasionally miss check-ins with those who needed them, or I didn't give attention or care to certain situations as much as some wished for. This led to hurt feelings, and while I did my best to make amends, some pastoral relationships would be forever changed going forward.

As these issues played out and piled up, I began to take note of my own reactions, some of which were becoming chronic more than situational. I especially noticed an ever-present tightness in my chest that would persist even if I was relaxing on the couch or lying in bed. I began doing more of my work at home, only venturing to the church building to pick up materials I needed or to make phone calls. And everything I was doing became tinged with an increasing amount of resentment and resignation. I was feeling perpetually tired and yet also perpetually anxious at the same time.

I was clearly in the decline stage of the call cycle at this point. It would take me a while to enter the evaluation/discernment stage. I had more immediate concerns about my mental and physical health, and I was able to identify several ways to address them. Among them was securing a prescription for Lexapro, which helped ease my physical symptoms of anxiety. The tightness in my chest went away after a few days on this medication, and I considered that a major positive development.

As to my feelings of fatigue and resentment, I was fortunate enough to have earned a sabbatical after five years of service, and it could not have come at a better time. I decided that the theme of this time away would be "falling back in love with my vocation," and I planned activities that would focus on rest, spiritual renewal, and reclarifying my own sense of call.

By the time my sabbatical began, I recognized that I had indeed entered evaluation/discernment. I had a hope that tending to my own needs would bring me to a time of reaffirmation and reengagement, but I left open the possibility that opting out might also be the best option for all involved.

IS IT BURNOUT?

When you believe that you have reached the evaluation and discernment stage of the call cycle, you may need to consider whether you have reached a mere dip in your energy and passion or whether you are experiencing something more serious and prolonged. Whatever our work, one's excitement for it will naturally experience peaks and valleys, which the call cycle is meant to illustrate. Acknowledging the inevitability of each will help us better prepare for their arrival and aid in our journey through them.

However, some situations, environments, or relationships will take a heavier toll on the minister. Maybe enough small setbacks, rejections, and instances of criticism absent their positive opposites will snowball over time. Maybe the demand for time, response, and attention becomes more than can be borne. Maybe the congregational system relies too heavily on the minister's energy for any kind of task to be planned or accomplished. Rather than a temporary decline in interest and energy, these sorts of situations may lead to something more serious known as burnout.

All who serve in ministry are bound to experience stress. At various times, stress is a normal companion to have in ministry. Certain seasons of the church's life that bring added responsibility or a heightened amount of change will cause ministers to feel more anxious and alert. For this reason, ministers are often encouraged to maintain routine self-care practices such as regularly taking time off, pursuing nonministry hobbies, prioritizing time with loved ones, and giving attention to holistic health.

Burnout is different from this normal presence of stress, and it can be detrimental to our entire selves as well as to our ministry. When going through a time of heightened stress, we may be able to step back from the factors in our lives that are causing it while reaching out to those practices that will help us restore balance.

Burnout not only threatens our energy level, but also our ability to continue finding meaning in what we're doing. This will include not only the primary factors that have led to this extreme point, but also the pastoral tasks on which we formerly were able to rely for reaffirmation and reengagement. Burnout disrupts the normal rhythms of the call cycle, leading us to a much more barren space within ourselves where any ministry task—-and ministry in general—no longer seems to matter.[5]

United Methodist Bishop Will Willimon once wrote about burnout in this way: "John Sandford suggests that the phenomenon of dissipation and disengagement, which we commonly call burnout, may arise from a lack of meaning rather than from a lack of energy. I agree. . . . In other words, people appear to burn out in the church not necessarily because they are overworked, but because they are overburdened with the trivial and the unimportant."[6]

While I find Willimon's definition helpful, I think that burnout may feature both a lack of energy and lack of meaning, as each contribute to the other. If ministers are no longer inspired by what they are doing, they will not draw from the energy that a consciousness of meaning would have provided. On the other hand, a constantly elevated demand on a minister's energy will lead to a decline in passion and meaning-making for one's work.

The causes of burnout will vary by individual and ministry context. However, some of the most common causes include:

- Overwork
- A lack of firm boundaries
- Taking responsibility for tasks or ministries that aren't yours
- A lack of regular rest and rejuvenation
- The weight of expectations from one's ministry context
- Trying to accomplish ministry tasks with inadequate resources
- A lack of support shown to the minister

As mentioned, burnout differs from stress in that it is more severe and tends to last much longer. There are also particular signs to watch for, including the following:

- A feeling of alienation from one's work
- Physical exhaustion
- Emotional exhaustion
- Spiritual exhaustion
- Reduced performance
- Increased cynicism about ministry tasks

- Heightened irritability
- Increased dependence on unhealthy coping mechanisms

While causes and signs of burnout may vary from case to case, methods of preventing or addressing burnout are relatively constant. The common thread that runs through all of them involves attentiveness to one's physical, mental, and spiritual health. These include:

- Maintaining balanced and nutritious eating habits
- Regular exercise
- Attention to mental health, including therapy and medication
- Maintaining spiritual health, such as a regular prayer practice or meeting with a spiritual director
- Regular check-ins with a support network, trusted colleagues, and mentors
- Taking regular time off
- Pursuing nonministry hobbies

In my own story, my most prominent burnout symptoms included a feeling of alienation (more work done from home), reduced performance, and an increase in cynicism and irritability. I was fortunate enough to have opportunities and resources at hand to begin addressing it, including going on medication and taking a sabbatical.

Of course, the causes, signs, and potential solutions for burnout will vary by individual, context, and available resources. And contrasted with normal amounts of stress, burnout may take much longer to address. But the importance of recognizing the signs and intentionally caring for oneself will always remain.

RULES FOR DISCERNMENT

In his *Spiritual Exercises*, Ignatius of Loyola wrote extensively about what he deemed the "discernment of spirits." This was his term for differentiating between the spiritual forces in our lives that may be guiding us toward or away from God's purposes and love. He recommends that we pay attention to our "interior movements:" the emotions, reactions, thoughts, and desires that are most prominent in our hearts and minds.[7] As part of this idea, he introduced the mirror concepts of spiritual consolation and spiritual desolation.

In spiritual consolation, one feels a close awareness of God's presence in their life. God's Spirit is easy to discern, and, as the name suggests, we feel consoled by this presence. If our interior movements bring us joy, peace, and gratitude, and lead us to positive, life-giving things, those are good additional signs that we are in a state of spiritual consolation.[8]

Spiritual desolation, as you might expect, is the opposite of spiritual consolation. In spiritual desolation, one feels distant from God. Our interior movements consist of inner turmoil, despair, anxiety, doubt, feeling as if we have no direction, and a tendency to make decisions that lead toward self-destruction.[9]

Spiritual desolation could be another term for burnout. These concepts share many of the same characteristics, and burnout does have a spiritual dimension as much as it has physical and mental dimensions. When one feels increasingly removed from one's work of ministry, that may also bring a feeling of alienation from God. Spiritual desolation, or burnout, not only applies to our work but affects our entire selves. Even if the former is the center of its onset, it will end up affecting the rest of who we are and what we do, including our self-image, our health, and our relationships.

In his explanation for the discernment of spirits, Ignatius advises against making any big life-changing moves when in a state of spiritual desolation. Any major change that one makes when in a state of desolation will be influenced by that state, and thus we may not be our best discerning selves when doing so. Rather than focusing on external changes, Ignatius advises that we focus on internal changes. We are first and foremost in need of healing our inward selves before we'll be in a healthier spiritual state to be making decisions that will affect our lives and the lives of those around us.[10]

Opting out of our current ministry may still be part of the answer when we reach the evaluation and discernment stage of the call cycle. However, to make a more clear-eyed, spiritually healthy decision, you will need a time of internal focus first. Otherwise, the risk of carrying our spiritual desolation and burnout into a new ministry setting becomes greater. If the environment of our ministry setting is so untenable that such healing cannot take place while remaining, it may be better to opt out without taking on new ministry responsibilities so as not to risk doing harm in a new ministry partnership.

One may not feel desolation or burnout in the evaluation and discernment stage but may nevertheless wonder if a time of low energy and inspiration may necessitate a change in ministry context. I've named a few ways to discern whether this is the case earlier in the chapter. First, consider the potential that the ministry partnership may still have. Could there still be more to do together if you stay, and, if so, what forms might that take? Second, revisit your shrines to remember that you are indeed called by God to ministry. This may in itself provide the reaffirmation you need to continue where you are or help provide direction and clarity if you still discern that opting out is for the best. Third, test the possibilities, including other potential settings. Depending on denominational polity, this may involve engaging in some interviews or speaking with your bishop. Even the act of having the conversation may provide insight into whether to stay or move on.

And now Ignatius has added a fourth caveat: pay attention to your interior movements. If you feel consoled by God's close presence, you are likely in a better state of mind and spirit to discern which path in the diverged journey to take.

Whatever form of discernment and consolation a minister needs, it always helps to count the stars with Abram, and remember God's calling and promise.

JOURNALING PRACTICE

1. Inhale a deep breath through the nose, and exhale through the mouth. Repeat this as many times as necessary to center yourself for the practice.
2. Draw a large circle and label parts of it with the different stages of the call cycle. Start with affirmation/engagement at the top and work your way around clockwise. Draw an arrow curving away from the part of the circle labeled evaluation/discernment, and label this arrow opting out.
3. Consider honestly and prayerfully where you currently are on the cycle. Reflect on the circumstances that may be contributing to your having reached that point. How are you feeling about where you are (e.g., satisfied, uncertain, tired, etc.)?

4. Revisit your journal entries for the Web of the Work and Practices for the Journey. How can these serve as resources at your current stage?
5. Repeat the breathing exercise until you feel moved to reenter your day. Give thanks to God for this time.

By the Grace of God

My sabbatical from the church brought the renewal and clarity that I hoped it would. This was due to the balance of rest and activity that I had planned for it, and several notable moments helped me as I worked out what to do next in this discernment and evaluation phase of ministry.

A close college friend reached out just as my time away began. He'd noticed that something had been up with me and invited me to meet at our undergrad alma mater to wander the campus and to talk. We spent time reminiscing, but he also gave me space to talk out what I'd been feeling about my vocation. The conversation was incredibly helpful, but so was just being at a favorite location with a good friend.

I spent some time at a retreat center, during which my experience of lying on the floor in the chapel taught me to listen to my body. I thought about the physical reactions I'd been having to circumstances at the church. While I was beginning to treat my anxiety, my internal state still brought questions of whether I'd need to recover from stress or if I had slipped into burnout.

I traveled to Pennsylvania to visit the grave of Rev. Anders Gustav Nelson, my ancestor whose life and ministry played a role in some of his descendants becoming ministers as well. The small clapboard church and adjacent cemetery along a winding county road were idyllic, and I felt inspired to stay at his grave for a while. I didn't know what to say while there, but I did express thankfulness for having finally made this trip.

I attended the United Church of Christ's General Synod, which perplexed friends and colleagues since it could technically be considered a work trip. But this gathering is always a chance to see so many people, and it feeds my spirit, so attendance isn't work to me. At one point near the end of the gathering, all UCC national staff were invited on stage for a moment of appreciation. I had often thought about a possible call to regional or national church work, but the right opportunity that would balance with my family's needs hadn't yet arisen. As I joined others in applause for the work these people do, I thought about whether I might someday be on that stage during such a moment myself.

Finally, I traveled with my family to Ormond Beach, Florida, for our annual vacation. I made it a point not to think about ministry much at all and instead allowed the sand and water refresh my body and spirit.

By the time my sabbatical ended, I'd received the rest that I long needed, and I had done a lot of necessary discernment and evaluation. And yet I still hadn't felt a clear path forward either toward reaffirmation or opting out. As much as I wished for a definitive sign, like Abram being shown the stars, I knew that such a thing no matter how small will arrive in its own time.

NOBODY ASKED FOR THIS

A year into the pandemic, I was tasked with analyzing data of ministers who'd resigned their positions to see if issues that had arisen had inspired a higher rate of people opting out of their roles. I pulled these numbers from the UCC Data Hub—at that time we had them for March 2020 through April 2021—and charted them month by month. To my surprise, there didn't seem to be a significant difference in comparison to the previous five years.[1]

I revisited this data the next year, thinking that there might be a greater difference. By this point, churches were beginning to meet in person again with many safety protocols in place, and, while things were still not as they were prior to March 2020, many ministry settings were beginning to find their footing to establish a new normal.

Surprisingly, there was again a drop in such resignations; taken in isolation, this seemed to be a positive development. Maybe this wasn't such a troublesome issue after all. However, something didn't sit right with me, and so I went back and also compiled the data of ministry positions added over the same period of time.

Here, finally, came a more complete picture of what has been happening: while the number of ministry resignations did not seem to be picking up, the number of ministers beginning in new positions was even lower, and had been for some time.[2] It appears as though the pool of candidates seeking to serve as pastors of congregations has been shrinking. My own conversations with conference staff across my denomination reveals that they are finding fewer candidates for open church positions, even for what would be considered the most desirable by conventional standards. No church is immune from this shortage.

As has been discussed throughout this book, the trends contributing to ministry's increased difficulty—and, apparently, its decreased appeal—have been unfolding for decades. When Lyle Schaller first used the term "unintentional interim" to describe challenging times of transition in ministry settings, it was an outlier, a strange anomaly that most ministers probably would not have to deal with over the course of their careers. In those days, sanctuaries were still full, budgets were still robust, and church involvement brought a beneficial social status for community members. During that first wave of interim ministry (and before), a minister could enjoy a relatively stable vocational journey from seminary graduation to retirement.[3]

Now in this third wave, however, "stable" may be one of the last words people in ministry use to describe their experiences. The surrounding culture has become much more transitional, and as a result ministry has as well. There is little wonder why not as many may be pursuing a call to serve God in this particular way, opting instead for explicit forms of ministry other than in congregations, or to practice what they still consider ministry outside the traditional boundaries of church and denominational structures.

In *The Church Cracked Open*, Stephanie Spellers speaks this truth plainly:

> No one asks to be cracked open or disrupted. No church seeks to decline in membership or stature. Most people don't go looking for experiences that will humble them and break their hold on treasured

> identity and culture. We did not choose to land here in this wilderness; we were shoved by pandemic, racial reckoning, decline, and economic and social disruption. But now that we're here, humbled and open, we have a choice and a chance.[4]

True enough, nobody who enters ministry asked to do so under these conditions. Nobody in ministry walks into a church expecting to be an unintentional interim, and yet it may not take very long to uncover a church's unresolved conflict, anxiety, and grief. At this point, as Spellers says, both minister and church have a choice and a chance: a choice to move through this unexpected transitional time as best and as far as they can, and a chance to move into a new beginning together, the minister succeeding themselves and writing a new chapter in the same corner of the body of Christ in which the previous one concluded. There is no guarantee that this will be the case, but the Holy Spirit is full of surprises, and a faithful shepherding through this time could yet bring another.

At this point, I want to return to the quote from Walter Brueggemann that I shared very early in this book: "The world for which you have been so carefully prepared is being taken away from you by the grace of God."[5] The first part of this quote is obvious enough. As Spellers notes, we are now in a time in which the effects of the pandemic are still with us, we continue to wrestle with the sinful heritage of America's violence and oppression toward nonwhite populations, and both churches and the wider culture are still figuring out how best to weather shifts in religious devotion and belonging. The world is changing, and what was once deemed more stable and desirable is being taken away from those seeking to devote their lives to the practice of ministry.

But the second part of the quote may cause us to wonder: how could we consider all this turmoil and upheaval "by the grace of God?"

Consider the world that many knew prior: a world of greater stability for the church, and yet also one of greater complacency. It was one of greater membership, but not necessarily of more faithful discipleship. It was one of higher worship attendance, but not necessarily one that welcomed those who looked, spoke, or loved outside of what was deemed acceptable.

Yes, with all this transition has come more anxiety, more anger, more of a longing for the past, more grief, more decline, more instability. And yet with it have also come opportunities for creativity, faithfulness, removing that which was no longer effective, increased ways for laypeople to use their gifts, opportunities to hold important conversations about participating in acts that will bring about more justice and inclusion for nonwhite and LGBTQ people.

Nobody asked for this. But now we have been given a choice and a chance to do ministry in some of the most critical times that churches have ever faced. Now we have a choice and a chance to experience and show one another God's gracious gifts of love, forgiveness, reconciliation, presence, and peace in ways unheard of to prior generations.

We may not yet have figured out what will replace this world being taken away, but, just as God pointed Abram toward the innumerable stars in the sky, God is also assuring us we will not do this work alone.

IT'S HOLY SATURDAY, BUT SUNDAY'S COMING

Of all the days on the Christian liturgical calendar, Holy Saturday may feel the most truthful to our life experience. It is the day after Good Friday, during which Jesus was crucified and laid in a tomb. His friends, loved ones, and followers were left to grieve and to make sense of what happened. This man who was a beloved companion and teacher and beacon of God's light to so many had been silenced by earthly power. That Rome had done so may not, on the one hand, have been much of a surprise: those with little status in the communities along the Sea of Galilee and Jordan River were likely used to such actions from their rulers. They'd perhaps seen the squashing of hope and reassertion of dominance before.

On the other hand, however, the life and preaching of this man Jesus had been different to them and had given them an alternative vision of the world. He had showed them the possibility of the type of community rooted in God's presence that could be one of peace rather than coercion, of love rather than violence, and of justice rather than inequality. Groups of followers likely had different ideas of how this vision would be brought into being, but he as the revealer of it all was showing them the way.

And now he was gone, thanks to their oppressors. And they were left to pick up the pieces.

On that first Holy Saturday, there was no feeling of inevitable celebration. There was no altar guild arranging lilies and tulips in the front of the sanctuary. There was no choir rehearsing their alleluias. There were no musicians preparing to lead people in singing "Christ the Lord is Risen Today." There was only mourning, loss, death, and wondering what to do next.

That is why I think Holy Saturday can feel so truthful to so many: because it's where so many people actually live. Whether due to estranged relationships, financial hardship, racist violence, discrimination due to gender identity or sexual orientation, the daily reality of war, the struggle to treat illnesses physical or mental, many feel the reality of being stuck in an in-between, Holy Saturday sort of existence. Tragedy or anxiety has visited, and there is not yet any indication that a resurrection experience will follow.

Even after the news of Jesus being raised by God began to spread at the end of the Gospels, we see so many instances of people hesitating to buy in to what their friends were sharing with them. At the end of Matthew, the disciples encounter the risen Christ, and while many fall down to worship, some still doubt (Matt. 28:17). In Mark, when the women who visit the tomb find it empty and are told about Jesus being raised, they flee in fear without telling anyone (Mark 16:8). When the women share the news of the empty tomb with the disciples in Luke, the disciples don't believe them (Luke 24:11).

Perhaps the most famous account of a disciple being slow to believe that resurrection has happened is that of Thomas in the Gospel of John. In John 20, the rest of the disciples are in a locked room together, and Jesus appears among them. Their natural instinct is to go inform the one who missed out, sharing their experience with Thomas and hoping that he would join in their celebration.

But it's still Holy Saturday for Thomas. He's never seen or experienced anything like what they're telling him about, and he is skeptical. Christian tradition likes to shame him for this, as if immediately believing that a person was raised from the dead and appeared in a locked room is the easiest thing to do. Instead, he responds that he wants his own experience, his own sign that this has happened. And he wants it to be so real for him that he has the option to stick his fingers in Jesus' wounds.

And so a week later, Thomas gets his wish. Jesus appears and even offers his hands in case he was serious about touching his wounds. Finally, Thomas has received his own sign, and he can join his fellow disciples in the wonder of this good news.

It may feel like Holy Saturday for many ministers and churches these days. This is an in-between time of transition where so much feels unsettled, and grief and uncertainty are guiding us more than hope and new life. This includes the large cultural shifts of our day, as well as cultural shifts that are happening more locally in communities and congregations. And Jesus doesn't seem to be appearing clear as day in any locked rooms to assuage our doubts and fears about the future of ministry or of the church.

Signs of resurrection tend to be much more subtle these days. They may come in a word shared during a pastoral visit. They may come through an appreciative email sent from a faithful online attendee from two states over. They may come through a newfound passion a group of members has for becoming more involved in local justice work. They may come through the slow making of peace with a concluded pastorate. They may come through a personal practice that helps you find renewal and reaffirmation for the work of ministry. They may come through the love and encouragement from one or more parts of your Web of the Work. Any of these signs, and so many others, may help move you from Holy Saturday despair to Easter Sunday rejoicing.

Because these signs are often so subtle, others may need help seeing and receiving them. The work of ministry has always included pointing out how and where God is present among the people; that has taken on a new urgency when so much transition swirls around a congregation from so many different sides and angles. The people of God are desperate to see and experience the possibility of resurrection as they navigate these strange times.

Just as ministers need signs for themselves, their people need them just as much. And wherever they occur, pointing them out will help renew hope for the future.

Ministry in transition is incredibly difficult. It's one thing to know that you are walking into such a situation, and quite another not to know until after you've observed for a while. Many of these transitions may be known given the events of recent years and decades, but some may have yet to be discovered. Whether one's ministry of transition is intentional or not, pointing out the signs of resurrection will be an enduring need. And if you don't know what else to do, that may be the place to begin.

AN EASTER FAREWELL

About a month after I returned from my sabbatical, I became aware of an opening at the UCC national setting. The position was for the sort of wider denominational work in which I've always been most interested: supporting others in ministry, particularly in areas of discernment and transition. This felt closer to the right opportunity than in past instances, and so I hurried to revise and submit my ministerial profile for consideration.

The interview process played out over the next few months. In the meantime, I continued to serve the church as best I could, although symptoms of anxiety and burnout persisted. But I continually told myself that if I was to remain in this type of ministry for the foreseeable future, I would do so at the level that the congregation needed and deserved.

The search committee offered me the position in early January of 2020, and I accepted. My resignation letter went out to the congregation shortly after. I'd remain pastor through the middle of April, and, as it happened, my final Sunday would be Easter.

Those intervening months provided opportunities for reflection regarding what had taken place over the seven years of our time together. I thought about that first day, which had presented a hard decision about whether to invite my predecessor back and had given the first hint that at least the first phase of our partnership would be to travel through the "neutral zone" toward a true beginning. I reflected on all the hard decisions that followed, as well as their imperfect results, and I resisted trying to conceive of better outcomes if I'd made different choices. I did feel some measure of confidence that we'd made some progress together: the church had moved through its grief, and while I was not going to be the one to benefit much from that, there would be a higher likelihood for my successors to do so.

I never actually applied the term "unintentional interim" to my experiences of this pastoral tenure until close to the very end. It's likely that a part of me was actively resisting doing so. After all, unintentional interims tend not to last as long as my time here had. And yet I could still see how moving the congregation through a time of transition that hadn't been resolved before I arrived was a feature of my ministry with them, and faithfulness to my vocation demanded that I attend to that.

In early March, I and many others began to get the sense of how serious this new virus in the news was becoming. In short succession, my martial arts dojo, our schools, and my new employer all announced that they were shutting down in-person activities. Not too long after, my Consistory president and I agreed that the church would need to do the same.

On Easter Sunday, I put on a clerical shirt and stole and preached my last sermon into my phone. I talked about resurrection hope in the face of despair and uncertainty. It was a message for me as much as it was for them, and I knew how much they'd need it, as these strange new circumstances didn't seem to be abating any time soon. I recognized and appreciated that this season of ministry would be challenging for ministers and churches in ways they'd never experienced.

A few days before this, I went to the church building to collect the few remaining items in my office. Before I left, however, I felt compelled to do one more thing: I walked down to the sanctuary and changed the paraments from Lenten purple to Easter white. The celebration of resurrection hadn't yet come, but it would eventually, and just as I'd tried my entire time there, I wanted to do this small action to help that happen for them. It wasn't much, but I thought that maybe this could be a sign that would give somebody hope in the months ahead.

In these times of transition, the best people in ministry can do is keep pointing to resurrection hope. Maybe the signs won't be big or obvious, and they may not yield the grand results that we expect or hope for. But as the old world for which we felt so prepared continues to pass away, they'll still be there, leading us into something new and glorious and life-giving, by the grace of God.

JOURNALING PRACTICE

1. Inhale a deep breath through the nose, and exhale through the mouth. Repeat this as many times as necessary to center yourself for the practice.
2. Divide a page with a line down the middle. Label one side Holy Saturday and the other Easter Sunday. List signs of each that are currently present in your ministry setting, including for yourself.

3. Consider each list, both what you specifically mentioned and how long each one is. Does anything stand out to you or surprise you? Is there anything on either list that you hadn't realized before this exercise?
4. Note any items on the Easter Sunday list that are giving you sustaining hope despite what might be on the Holy Saturday list. Ponder ways to keep it close to you as your ministry continues to unfold.
5. Repeat the breathing exercise until you feel moved to reenter your day. Give thanks to God for this time.

Last Things

My own "unintentional interim" story ends near the beginning of the pandemic. As such, I acknowledge that it may not have much in common with such stories that have played out since that time. Even years later, the effects of COVID-19 are still making themselves known in churches and in the wider world, and congregations as a result are experiencing a unique combination of grief and uncertainty. So a minister may decide that their ministry may not be for the long term, but perhaps for reasons other than what led to my own discernment.

In my current work, I am certainly privy to ministers' experiences with how congregations have expressed their reactions to transitional anxiety in harmful, destructive, traumatizing, nonaffirming ways. These attitudes and behavior are often directed toward their pastor, making them the scapegoat, and the pastor in response makes the best choice for the sake of their own health to move on. So in that sense, my story may differ from others' as well (one in such a case may be able to relate more to the story of the phone call that my family received).

Unintentional interims will take an inevitable toll on the minister who finds themselves serving in this capacity. While I've shared some practices to care for one's well-being while serving in such a role, I admit that I haven't spent time in this book exploring the need to process this experience after that ministry is concluded. There are likely to be lingering effects to which you may need to attend even after your time of leaving. This reality is not to be ignored or downplayed, and you will need people from your Web of the Work to do this important, ongoing work of healing. If you have happened upon this book near or after the end of such a ministry experience, I pray that you are able to get what you need.

These transitional times are redefining what it looks like to serve in ministry. You likely don't need me to tell you that, as you have firsthand knowledge of this truth through your own lived experience. I suspect that we will be trying to define the particulars for some time to come. And just as we think we've begun to figure it out, things will likely change again.

However the particulars of transition might change from one month, one year, one generation to the next, the work of guiding ministry settings through it will not. And neither will a minister's own need for faithful discernment; practices for one's own health; giving space for disillusionment, grief, and negative expectations; and relying on a network of trusted voices. The demands of ministry will always necessitate attention to oneself in order to be faithful, effective, and whole.

My wish for you, the reader, is that you pursue that attention as best as you are able and however you need to do so. By the grace of God, may signs of resurrection always be found, because we will always need them for this call that we have received.

Acknowledgements

This book has been more than eighteen years in the making. Some of the concepts discussed in this book have been percolating for that long and have taken various forms in conversations and presentations and other pieces of writing that I've produced over that timeframe. As such, they also have many fingerprints on them via feedback, refinement, influence, and inspiration, and I'm grateful to those who have helped provide that.

Thank you first to Rachel Hackenberg, Katie Martin, and the entire staff at the Pilgrim Press for their partnership. I am grateful for the opportunity.

Thanks to David Grandouiller for your guidance and suggestions through the developmental editing process.

Thank you to Michele Bagby Allan, Dave Sigmund, and Joey Feldmann for being among my first beta testers for this material, even though none of us knew it at the time. Thank you to Susie Bjork as well for your collaboration.

Mindy Quellhorst, George Miller, Jeanne Murawski, Alex and Hope Molozaiy, and Brian Burke have been longtime faithful friends, colleagues, and partners in discernment.

To my colleagues on the Ministerial Excellence, Support, and Authorization Team—Elizabeth Dilley, Anissa Glaser-Bacon, Tara Barber, Melanie

Oommen, Renee Jackson, Stephen Boyd, Darrell Ludwig, Tanika Wainwright—I am so glad to partner with you in ministry.

Thanks to Ian Borton, communications professor extraordinaire, who has accompanied me on many walks around Heidelberg University and elsewhere while I've tried to figure things out.

The staff at Artisan Coffee Shop provide delicious coffee and cinnamon rolls, as well as a wonderful atmosphere that I've enjoyed while writing every book I've ever published.

I'm always grateful for my family's love, support, and encouragement.

Bibliography

AJMC Staff. "A Timeline of COVID-19 Developments in 2020." *The American Journal of Managed Care*, January 1, 2021. Online, https://www.ajmc.com/view/a-timeline-of-covid19-developments-in-2020, accessed September 26, 2022.

Barry, William A. *Finding God in All Things: A Companion to the Spiritual Exercises of St. Ignatius*. Notre Dame: Ave Maria, 2008.

Beaumont, Susan. *How to Lead When You Don't Know Where You're Going: Leading in a Liminal Season*. Lanham, MD: Rowman & Littlefield, 2019.

Beck, Martha. *Finding Your own North Star: Claiming the Life You Were Meant to Live*. New York: Three Rivers, 2001.

Bell, Rob. *Jesus Wants to Save Christians: A Manifesto for the Church in Exile*. Grand Rapids: Zondervan, 2008.

Bendroth, Norman. *Interim Ministry in Action: A Handbook for Churches in Transition*. Lanham, MD: Rowman & Littlefield, 2018.

Bendroth, Norman, ed. *Transitional Ministry Today: Successful Strategies for Churches and Pastors*. Lanham, MD: Rowman & Littlefield, 2015.

Bridges, William, with Susan Bridges. *Managing Transitions: Making the Most of Change*. Boston: Da Capo, 2016.

Brueggemann, Walter. *Genesis*. Atlanta: John Knox, 1982.

Boers, Arthur Paul. *Never Call Them Jerks: Healthy Responses to Difficult Behavior*. Washington, D.C.: Rowman and Littlefield, 1999.

Burkeman, Oliver. *Four Thousand Weeks: Time Management for Mortals*. New York: Farrar, Strauss & Giroux, 2021.

Cook, Brian. "The Black Pit of Negative Expectations." *MGoBlog*, September 3, 2018. Online, https://mgoblog.com/content/black-pit-negative-expectations, accessed February 14, 2022.

del Toro, Guillermo. *Cabinet of Curiosities: My Notebooks, Collections, and Other Obsessions*. New York: Harper Design, 2013.

Delk, Yvonne, ed. *Afro-Christian Convention: The Fifth Stream of the United Church of Christ*. Cleveland: Pilgrim, 2023.

Fretheim, Terence E. "The Book of Genesis: Introduction, Commentary, and Reflections," *The New Interpreter's Bible, Vol. I*. Ed. Leander E. Keck et al. Nashville: Abingdon, 1994. 319-674.

Gabriel, Chris. "July 2019," UCC *COMma*, July 16, 2019, online, https://www.ucc.org/comma_july_2019/, accessed January 25, 2023.

Hamm, Richard L. *Recreating the Church: Leadership for the Postmodern Age*. St. Louis: Chalice, 2007.

Horsley, Richard A. *1 Corinthians*. Nashville: Abingdon, 1998.

Ivens, Michael. *Understanding the Spiritual Exercises*. Herefordshire: Gracewing, 2008.

Kleon, Austin. *Keep Going: 10 Ways to Stay Creative in Good Times and Bad*. New York: Workman, 2019.

Kruzman, Diana. "Houses of worship grapple with the future of their online services." *Religion News Service*, February 14, 2022. Online, https://religionnews.com/2022/02/14/houses-of-worship-grapple-with-the-future-of-their-online-services/, accessed September 26, 2022.

Long, Thomas G. *The Witness of Preaching*, 2nd ed. Louisville: Westminster John Knox, 2005.

Ludwig, Glenn E. *In It for the Long Haul: Building Effective Long-Term Pastorates*. Bethesda: Alban, 2002.

Marich, Jamie and Anna Pirkl. *Transforming Trauma with Jiu-Jitsu: A Guide for Survivors, Therapists, and Jiu-Jitsu Practitioners for Facilitate Embodies Recovery*. Berkeley: North Atlantic, 2022.

Merton, Thomas. *New Seeds of Contemplation*. New York: New Directions, 1972.

Nelson, Jeff. "Trends in Ministry Resignations." *A Statistical Profile 2022*. UCC Center for Analytics, Research & Development, and Data, Cleveland, 2022.

Nelson, Jeff. "The Pandemic's Effects on Ministry Resignations." *A Statistical Profile 2021*. UCC Center for Analytics, Research & Development, and Data, Cleveland, 2021.

Niebuhr, Reinhold. *Leaves from the Notebook of a Tamed Cynic*. Louisville: Westminster John Knox, 1990.

O'Brien, Kevin. *The Ignatian Adventure: Experiencing the Spiritual Exercises of Saint Ignatius in Daily Life*. Chicago: Loyola, 2011.

Packard, Joshua. "Meet the Dones." *Christianity Today*, July 6, 2015. Online, https://www.christianitytoday.com/pastors/2015/summer-2015/meet-dones.html, accessed September 26, 2022.

Pallardy, Richard. "First Day of Fall." *Britannica*. Online, https://www.britannica.com/story/first-day-of-fall, accessed September 14, 2022.

Peterson, Eugene. *Under the Unpredictable Plant: An Exploration in Vocational Holiness*. Grand Rapids: William B. Eerdmans, 1992.

PRRI Staff. "2021 PPRI Census of American Religion, Updates and Trends: White Christian Decline Slows, Unaffiliated Growth Levels Off," April 27, 2022. Online, https://www.prri.org/spotlight/prri-2021-american-values-atlas-religious-affiliation-updates-and-trends-white-christian-decline-slows-unaffiliated-growth-levels-off/, accessed September 26, 2022.

Schaller, Lyle E. *Survival Tactics in the Parish*. Nashville: Abingdon, 1977.

Spellers, Stephanie. *The Church Cracked Open: Disruption, Decline, and New Hope for Beloved Community*. New York: Church Publishing, 2021.

Taylor, Barbara Brown. *Leaving Church: A Memoir of Faith*. San Francisco: HarperSanFrancisco, 2006.

White, James Emery. "They're Not Coming Back." *Church & Culture*, March 28, 2022. Online, https://www.churchandculture.org/blog/2022/3/28/theyre-not-coming-back, accessed September 26, 2022.

Xenakis, Christopher. "Homesteading: What Does it Mean When Authorized UCC Ministers Don't Move?" *Vital Signs and Statistics*, June 12, 2017. Online, https://carducc.wordpress.com/2017/06/12/homesteading-what-does-it-mean/, accessed November 17, 2022.

Endnotes

Chapter 1

1. Norman Bendroth, "Whither Transitional Ministry?", in *Transitional Ministry Today* (Lanham, MD: Rowman & Littlefield, 2015), 4.
2. Lyle E. Schaller, *Survival Tactics in the Parish* (Nashville: Abingdon, 1977), 29.
3. AJMC Staff, "A Timeline of COVID-19 Developments in 2020," *The American Journal of Managed Care* (January 1, 2021), online, lines 13, 43, 63.
4. Diana Kruzman, "Houses of Worship Grapple with the Future of Their Online Services," *Religion News Service*, February 14, 2022, online, lines 20–24.
5. James Emery White, "They're Not Coming Back," *Church & Culture*, March 28, 2022, online, lines 9–11.
6. PRRI Staff, "2021 PPRI Census of American Religion, Updates and Trends," figures 1, 4.
7. Joshua Packard, "Meet the Dones," *Christianity Today*, July 6, 2015, online, lines 6–9.
8. Stephanie Spellers, *The Church Cracked Open* (New York: Church Publishing, 2021), 20–21.
9. Barbara Brown Taylor, *Leaving Church* (San Francisco: Harper, 2006), 122.
10. Schaller, *Survival Tactics*, 29–30.

Chapter 2

1. Reinhold Neibuhr, *Leaves from the Notebook of a Tamed Cynic* (Louisville: Westminster John Knox, 1990), 74.
2. Eugene Peterson, *Under the Unpredictable Plant* (Grand Rapids: William B. Eerdmans, 1992), 16–17.

Chapter 3

1. Brian Cook, "The Black Pit of Negative Expectations," *MGoBlog*, September 3, 2018, online, lines 18–43.

2. Richard Horsley, *1 Corinthians* (Nashville: Abingdon, 1998), 114.

Chapter 4

1. I recognize that not all readers are fans of nontraditional forms of worship. I encourage you to stick with the story for its larger purpose.

2. William Bridges with Susan Bridges, *Managing Transitions* (Boston: Da Capo, 2016), 7–8.

3. Ibid., 5.

4. Richard Pallardy, "First Day of Fall," *Britannica*, online, lines 1–7.

5. Oliver Burkeman, *Four Thousand Weeks* (New York: Farrar, Strauss & Giroux, 2021), 20–21.

Chapter 5

1. Bendroth, "Whither Transitional Ministry?", 4.

2. Norman Bendroth, *Interim Ministry in Action* (Lanham, MD: Rowman & Littlefield, 2018), 85.

3. Ibid.

4. Ibid.

5. Yvonne Delk, ed., *Afro-Christian Convention* (Cleveland: The Pilgrim Press, 2023).

6. Bendroth, *Interim Ministry in Action*, 87.

7. Susan Beaumont, *How to Lead When You Don't Know Where You're Going* (Lanham, MD: Rowman & Littlefield, 2019), 24.

8. Rob Bell, *Jesus Wants to Save Christians* (Grand Rapids: Zondervan, 2008), 166.

9. Bendroth, *Interim Ministry in Action*, 91.

10. Beaumont, *How to Lead*, 116.

11. Ibid.

12. Bendroth, *Interim Ministry in Action*, 96.

13. Richard Hamm, *Recreating the Church* (St. Louis: Chalice, 2007), 37.

14. Bendroth, *Interim Ministry in Action*, 96.

15. Ibid.

16. Beaumont, *How to Lead*, 116.

Chapter 6

1. This group may go by a different name in your congregation. This was our group that assists the minister with spiritual matters in the church such as pastoral care concerns, helping steward the sacraments, and so on.

2. Thomas G. Long, *The Witness of Preaching*, 2nd ed. (Louisville: Westminster John Knox, 2005), 26.

3. Ibid., 15.

4. Chris Gabriel, "July 2019," *UCC COMma*, July 16, 2019, online, lines 6–16.

Chapter 7

1. Eugene Peterson, *Under the Unpredictable Plant* (Grand Rapids: Eerdmans, 1992), 16.

2. Ibid.

3. Christopher Xenakis, "Homesteading: What Does It Mean When Authorized UCC Ministers Don't Move?" Vital Signs and Statistics blog, June 12, 2017, online, lines 14–15.

4. Glenn Ludwig, *In It for the Long Haul* (Bethesda, MD: Alban, 2002), 39–62.

Chapter 8

1. This book, *Coffeehouse Contemplative: Spiritual Direction for the Everyday*, was published in 2016 and is available through Noesis Press, an imprint of the Davies Group Publishers.

2. Arthur Paul Boers, *Never Call Them Jerks* (Washington, D.C.: Rowman and Littlefield, 1999), 57–58.

3. Ibid., 60.

4. Jamie Marich and Anna Pirkl, *Transforming Trauma with Jiu-Jitsu* (Berkeley, CA: North Atlantic, 2022), 28–31.

5. Martha Beck, *Finding Your Own North Star* (New York: Three Rivers, 2001), 116–17.

6. Ibid.,109–10.

7. Kevin O'Brien, *The Ignatian Adventure* (Chicago: Loyola, 2011), 69.

8. William Barry, *Finding God in All Things* (Notre Dame: Ave Maria, 2008), 34.

9. Thomas Merton, *New Seeds of Contemplation* (New York: New Directions, 1972), 216.

10. Guillermo del Toro, *Cabinet of Curiosities* (New York: Harper Design, 2013), 11.

11. Austin Kleon, *Keep Going* (New York: Workman, 2019), 105.

Chapter 9

1. Terence Fretheim, "The Book of Genesis," in *The New Interpreter's Bible*, Vol. I, ed. Leander E. Keck et al. (Nashville: Abingdon, 1994), 445.

2. Walter Brueggemann, *Genesis* (Atlanta: John Knox, 1982), 144.

3. Ibid.

4. I reflect more on communal discernment in my book *Coffeehouse Contemplative*.

5. Ludwig, *In It for the Long Haul*, 41.

6. Ibid., 40.

7. O'Brien, *The Ignatian Adventure*, 115.

8. Ibid., 117.

9. Ibid.

10. Michael Ivens, *Understanding the Spiritual Exercises* (Herefordshire: Gracewing, 2008), 219.

Chapter 10

1. Jeff Nelson, "The Pandemic's Effect on Ministry Resignations," A Statistical Profile 2021, UCC Center for Analytics, Research & Development, and Data, Cleveland, 2021, 58–59.

2. Jeff Nelson, "Trends in Ministry Resignations," A Statistical Profile 2022, UCC Center for Analytics, Research & Development, and Data, Cleveland, 2022, 50–52.

3. I must acknowledge the caveat that, in mainline traditions, this stability was enjoyed almost exclusively by ministers who presented as straight white men. And while progress has been made thanks in part to these more transitional times and cultural shifts, churches' willingness to consider ministry candidates whose identity diverges in one or more ways from this "norm" has expanded but is still relatively limited, even in spaces that consider themselves welcoming, affirming, and diverse.

4. Spellers, *The Church Cracked Open*, 133.

5. Taylor, *Leaving Church*, 122.